UNDEFENDABLE

THE STORY OF A TOWN UNDER FIRE

Edited by Sulari Gentill & Sarah Kynaston

Clan Destine
PRESS

First published by Clan Destine Press in 2022
PO Box 121,
Bittern Victoria 3918
Australia

National Library of Australia Cataloguing-In-Publication data:
Editors: Sulari Gentill & Sarah Kynaston
Undefendable: the story of a town under fire

ISBNs: 978-0-6453168-7-2 (hardcover)
       978-0-6453168-8-9 (paperback)

Photos by the townspeople of Batlow, New South Wales
Cover photos: The Brown family
Cover design by Willsin Rowe
Design & Typesetting by Clan Destine Press

Clan Destine
P R E S S

www.clandestinepress.net

To all those who came to our aid,
who stood with us in person and in thought.
We saw you, we heard you,
we knew you were there.

Contents

Introduction

The summer of 2019-2020 was a stage set for disaster. Drought, climate change, soaring temperatures, heatwave after heatwave. Australians are used to hot summers, but there was something different about this year.

The fire season started early and soon it seemed Australia was ablaze. But that summer spawned a new creature, a kind of burning juggernaut we'd not seen before. A fire so immense it created its own weather system.

Of course, even megablazes must have a beginning, a point of ignition. The Dunns Road Fire had its beginnings in a lightning strike on Boxing Day. And from that point it grew, jumping into the forests and devouring all the country before it as it raced towards the mountains.

As the front burned its way south-west, all those in its path prepared to protect their homes. The eyes of the world were on Australia, amazed that walls of flame were being met by volunteers. Experts mapped the fire systems, warned, and declared disaster.

And Batlow, a small town in the Snowy Mountains, was deemed undefendable.

This is the story of that town, told by its people. Those who fought, those who evacuated, those who lost and those who saved and were saved. This is a collection of personal accounts told in the words of ordinary people. They may not be a work of literary greatness, but they are honest and sincere — the stories of Batlownians, their memories, their pain, their gratitude. It is the little things we didn't share with the world media, the connections that locals understand, the defiance and the humour that got us through Black Summer and beyond.

It is us, in our words, and our pictures.

Sulari Gentill and Sarah Kynaston

The Hills

Kathryn Masterson

The Hills
And their story
Of a snake
From the sky

The Hills
And their patterns
From the past
Truth lies

Sulari on Kathryn Masterson

Kathryn is a relative newcomer to Batlow, but she has embraced the town wholeheartedly with her natural warmth and enthusiasm.

Kate has settled here with her son, planting and building on a property she's called Endor.

She has an eye for potential and beauty and has found both in Batlow.

For Those Who Fought

Frank Steenholt

From out of the West it came in those hot early January days
When Hell's gates were flung open and the demons forged through
   with fire, smoke and fear for those in their way.
As the fires burned and the grouser plates turned,
As the earth was bared and the firebreaks cut in,
The people of the highlands rose up to face the beast.

But the beast was strong and we all fell back to start again
Fires kept burning, grousers kept turning and again we fell back.
Everyone hoped it would be held on the ridge,
   but the fires burned on in their unending quest

They came from near and far to lend us a hand,
   the sons and daughters of the Great South Land
Thank goodness they did for the thing had grown far too big
   for a small group of locals to fight on our own.
'How far has it gone?' they asked.
Well, we didn't know.
'The town's undefendable!' the experts declared,
   'so we think it's best that you all go.'
Still the fires burned but the good people of the high ground said 'No!'
'This is our town and these are our homes and for them we will fight!'
And fought they did.

They gave it all they had but sadly not all could be saved
The beast was too strong on that terrible day
It came into the town with the roar of a jet
Everyone stood their ground and gave it their best

Fires still burn and grousers still turn
And the people stood up and stood tall
But how much longer can we we go on?

We've not slept for days but there's still work to be done,
There's no end in sight, it just keeps on coming.
So we keep refilling the step-ons, top-up the fuel in the pumps.
We're all dead on our feet but the fight must go on
We can sleep when it's over, now's not the time
For now we must run to chase down and black out the many spot fires
Wet down the burning trees, the logs, and the stumps
We've saved too much ground to risk losing it all now.

By the end of the week the battle was won.
We should all feel proud of the job that's been done.
It's time now to reflect on things that have been
and try to block out some of the horrors I've seen.

When you see the firefighters just shake their hands and say:
    'Thank you friends, for the great service that you have all done'.
And I for one will not forget just how honoured I felt
    to have fought beside a small group of such bloody good men.
When the call to battle comes again
As we know well, it will,
We will answer the call.
Some may be too old — it's a job for younger men.
But if it comes in my time, I know deep inside,
That when the fires of summer burn and the grousers again turn
We will all rise up and do it all again.

Sulari on Frank Steenholt

Frank Steenholt is my neighbour. He lives in the house in which he was raised, on the family property on Old Tumbarumba Road. Frank began his education in the one-teacher school that would one day become my house, and he will tell you that he is still learning. A fossicker, an inventor, a bushman and now a poet, Frank defended his home against Dunns Road, marshalling a small but tenacious army which included his sister, his brother-in-law, his nephew and a young man from across the road. With bulldozers and drip torches, they faced the full force of the front.

It was seeing what was going on next door in the days before the fire reached us, that convinced me to evacuate. The sheer scale of the neighbours' preparations gave me an idea of what was coming and made me realise that it was not something we could meet with a 1000L pod on an old Bedford truck. Frank's Army was putting in place a fire plan that would have made Eisenhower proud.

In the blackened aftermath when we were all dealing with ruins and ashes, spot fires and falling trees, Frank showed me an old exercise book in which he'd scribbled down a few thoughts about what had happened. And the idea for this anthology was born.

Origins of the Batlow RFS   Fred Fairlie

Fred Fairlie
Fred was born and bred in Batlow and has lived in the town for the whole of his 91 years. His family have been established in Batlow since the early 1900s and lived out of town along with the Browns who were his aunt's family.

   He was an active member of the town's firefighting crew in the early days and shared his memories.

'They had no worry whatsoever of fire because they were that conscious of it in those days. Up around the mill, Brown's Mill they called it, all the bush was cleared. You used to drive a sulky through with no worry about scrub or anything'. Fred laughed as he clarified, 'You can't say car because there weren't any around. But you could drive a sulky with no worries. No blackberries whatsoever back then.

   'The fire situation was pretty stable in all the following years. Before the 1950s the town water came from an old miner's race, and all we had was a hose reel on sulky wheels, but once the town had piped water and hydrants we formed the brigade. The fire siren was on the wall of the RSL and could be heard all over town. They rang the siren and then had to wait there until we came and found out where to go.

   'The town brigade did the rural fighting stuff as well because the Rurals only had a knapsack and beaters, that's all they had. We had a 200 gallon tank on the old Blitz and we'd go out to fires. I can remember one occasion, we went out to Kunama, and we only had the big pump. I stood in the dam to hold the hose up so it

didn't go down in the mud. If it dropped down in the mud, it would suck the mud through and make it useless. So I was up to my waist in water holding the fire hose to get the pump to work.

'Another occasion, the same thing, the town brigade went out to where Greg Mouat lives. It was Christmas Day 1966. Greg was only a little boy and he and his brother were fighting over what they were going to do. Greg said we were very happy.' Fred laughed. 'We were all having Christmas dinner with a few beers when the alarm went off!' Again we only had a small amount of water and could only do the speed the reel was capable of, but we kept the fire under control.

'From there it got better and better, the NSW Fire Commission took over in 1967 and the RFS formed.

'Roy Free organised a Rural Fire competition between all the shires, Tumut, Tumbarumba, right down as far as Ournie. We took part in that for about three years and then they abandoned it. But we won both the Tumut Shire Shield which is still down in the fire station. Also the Sir William Hudson Shield, it's down there too.

'To see what you can spend on equipment, and what you DON'T need to put out a fire. For instance the Snowy had massive pumps for fire, and we had that old Blitz with just a 200 gallon thing on the back. But the men who operated it, they were first-class bushmen. They were top chainsaw men, they were axemen, virtually champion axe and chainsaw men and cool-headed, and we could just personally beat the big equipment. They knew how to go about the job and clear stuff. The driver of the Blitz, Morrie Adams, he could put it through a sheep yard, a big vehicle and he could back up and be around and gone.'

After reminiscing Fred turned to the recent fire. Sadly he had only recently lost his wife.

'My son's got a unit down at Bermagui, and he'd taken me down there for a bit of a break. While we were down there Cobargo burnt out, all right through to Bega. It all got burned and we were there for that and had to evacuate from Bermagui down to Merimbula. We were sleeping in the car for a couple of nights, until they gave us the okay to get out. But we only had an hour to get out to Bega and then through to Cooma. We got to Cooma and we couldn't come any further. We had to get to Batlow through Canberra. There was fire or thick smoke most of the way.

'At that stage the fire here — well it hadn't started really to be the ferocious fire it ended up. We were home for a couple of days, and then next thing we were told to get out of Batlow. We were told it was undefendable but sheer determination by the brigade and locals saved Batlow. My house survived, big bark embers came down from the hill but they were mostly out by the time they reached my place.

'Once the petrol station exploded there didn't seem much hope of saving anything at that stage with it being so close in to town. But it was mostly outlying homes that got burnt. Other than that we were lucky we came out of it.'

How close is that fire?

Margaret Sedgwick

Monday the 30th December, 2019 was an ordinary day. I was aware of the fire raging in the forests at Ellerslie, but it appeared to be reasonably far away and not of major concern to me or most other Batlow residents.

I live three kms south of Batlow. That night I was reading in bed, preparing to put out the light about 10.30 when my mobile pinged with a message from Fires Near Me — an alert to be prepared for evacuation.

Evacuation? Incredible? How could that be? I quickly got dressed, putting on jeans, long sleeved shirt and boots and went outside on my back verandah. I could scarcely believe what I saw. To the west, the horizon was a wall of flames, brilliant red, orange — the sky was on fire. It was so frightening — I had never seen anything like it. I had no idea how close it was — one kilometre or ten, but it looked close, it looked threatening.

I decided that I would sleep in my chair, setting an alarm to wake me every hour, so I

could be aware of the approaching fire. But I couldn't sleep, going outside every ten or so minutes to look at the western sky, with alerts from the Fires Near Me app regularly coming through.

Sometime after midnight, I gave up trying. I was restless, scared, constantly looking up the Fires Near Me app, and watching the fire from my verandah. I did have a fire plan of sorts and I started to pack some precious belongings: paintings, photo albums and pictures into boxes, baskets etc. Clothes went into a suitcase, some memorabilia and valuables were carefully packed into a clothes basket, and then I started to pack these into my car.

It must be appreciated that I was/am uncomfortable about going into the darkness, so it's an indication of how terrified I was of the fire that I didn't hesitate to go outside to the garage to pack the car. I also went up the driveway to turn off the gas bottles — not knowing much about gas, I hoped I was turning the knob the right way.

So what to do now? It was then 1am, maybe even 1.30 am and I thought too late to knock on the doors of neighbours, friends. I decided my best option was to drive into Batlow, find somewhere to park my car and spend the night in the car. I drove around town, looking for likely places to park and settled on the carpark of the Apple Inn motel.

I had company at the motel. Two men who had been planning to attend the Tumbarumba Rodeo on New Year's Day, were also anxious; smoking and drinking endless cups of coffee while wandering around the motel parking area.

If anyone has ever tried to sleep in a car, especially when the adrenalin is high and one is so nervous, the fact that I had only about 30 minutes sleep will not surprise.

Dawn and 6am came as a relief. We were safe, for at least that night. I drove around town at that early hour and discovered other 'refugees' from Kunama who had also spent the night in their cars. We were tired, needed a shower and nourishment but at least we had survived that night.

I evacuated that day.

Sulari on Margaret Sedgwick

Margaret Sedgwick OAM came to Batlow as a newlywed, settling at Jilba where she and her husband Dick raised three daughters and became the backbone of the Batlow Community. Every committee, every fundraiser, every issue that affected the town or its people was led, supported or advocated by Margaret. She speaks thoughtfully, with a kind of gentle refinement, commanding respect and inspiring warmth. Margaret has run street stalls, made sandwiches, chaired meetings and lobbied parliament. For many years she was the Flower Steward of the Batlow Show, a position which requires experience and energy and elegance.
   And all those things speak of Margaret Sedgwick.

A Hell of a Shock

Bob and Jenny Bowman

Bob: We left Christmas Eve. No, New Year's Eve I think it was. We went up to our daughter's. I felt that there was no point in staying because we would only be in the way and if we were gone there would be one less place to have to worry about. We shut the house up and hoped for the best. We had cleared around pretty well and so on and we just left for Cobar.

Jenny: I had a hip replacement two or three weeks before this so I wouldn't have been much use. As it was I could only drive to Tumut.

Bob: She wasn't supposed to be driving but we had two cars.

Jenny: It wasn't really that bad.

Bob: So we left one car in Tumut and took the other to Cobar. While we were up there Rob, our Grandson, picked up the radio frequency the fire comms and it came through that the big pines on Keenans Road were alight.

I said, 'that's it, we'll have nothing to go home for'. So we listened and listened and then they... they did such a fantastic job.

Jenny: We were there a couple of weeks, I think.

Bob: No, wasn't a couple of weeks, it was a few days. As soon as they opened the road I came back because I was here for two or three days with the generators and that going. Sarah came down and cleaned our freezer out for us. We thought everything was right, then a few days later I could smell something. She'd thought the bread might be all right but the meat had dripped into it and it had all gone rotten.

Impressions when they came back

Jenny: It was a hell of a shock

Bob: Yeah I couldn't believe it. In all the years I have lived here. I saw places I have never seen because of all the forest. It was like the area opened up all at once and there was just vast areas of nothing.

Jenny: Russell brought up a thing on his computer about the Wybalena being burned and it was absolutely tragic. It was a lovely house.

Bob: It was a show piece of Batlow, with those old stables.

Jenny: And lots of workers.

Jenny: It was incredible wasn't it the way it must have swept along that valley with all those new houses..

Bob: How any of those houses out that way survived you'd never know.

Jenny: It's just amazing. Well I mean look at the garages that burnt and the old places standing right next to it. Or just one house out of a row of houses...gone.

Bob: There's no doubt about it, the RFS did a fantastic job. Really I am surprised how much of it survived.

Jenny: But we came back, it was never ever a thought not to.

Bob: It was a foregone conclusion when the fire came in.

Jenny: I never expected the house to go I don't think. Worry about it when it happens maybe.

Is there something unusual about the makeup of the RFS right now?

Before...

Bob: Back in 1986 we had fires and we went for the fortnight. I think we were home for about two hours. You were just racing from one spot to the other. You just didn't stop. Bad storm season.

Jenny: Forestry was a bit more active in those days.

Bob: I reckon that if forestry had been as well equipped now as they were at that stage it would never have got to the stage it was.

Jenny: I mean they sold everything, the fire trails were blocked... well they sold everything off didn't they, the workshop, the workforce. The headquarters...

The old days

Bob: It was back in the 40s they first started.

Jenny: Of course you weren't in it in the 40s.

Bob: I didn't join it actually...It wasn't that sort of structured thing.

Jenny: People just rocked up if or when they were available.

Bob: There was no formal training. I remember the first fire for our local, I must have been 14 or 15. All we had were wet bags and bushes. You'd just tear a bit off a tree.

Jenny: Not tried putting a fire out that way? You drop a match in a pouch of grass and it goes further than you expect.

Why small communities like Batlow always had an RFS.

Jenny: We're surrounded by all these pine trees.

Bob: You sort of help out. If it is burning on your neighbour's place, it is much better to fight it on his place than wait for it to get to yours! It was straight out voluntary.

Jenny: It was the days when things were done by volunteers, I mean, the ambulance lot, they were just people. Barry Smith, he was with them. They'd go to every football match and be there with a presence. And when the hospital opened Rossie Rosslow used to take x-rays and he had no formal training really. He was self-taught in a way. On the weekend you might have to wait while he finished his round of golf and then he'd come and take an x-ray, but you got treatment, there and then. No going off to Wagga in a creaking old bloody ambulance which was a horrible experience. You think it is going to disintegrate, actually.

Bob: You had to make do with virtually no equipment. Then they got to and bought things. The first equipment we got were old tin knapsacks. Copper tops. They get hot. They had beaters that were like hands with flat leather piece on the end.

Jenny: We used to have a major street stall every year and Gary Price was involved and he'd get the growers' agents in Sydney to send stuff so we'd have a stack of fruit and vegetables and everything. That was a really good money raiser, wasn't it?

Bob: Things sort of started off and they slowly built up and then during the years of the Snowy they started running the bushfire comps. That was when it really took off. They ran a competition here to start with and, well, Batlow didn't even have a tanker. We had a truck and for months before we spent nights down in the forestry workshop building it and we built this tank and that is what all those cups that are in the fire shed are for.

Jenny: Batlow unfortunately won it too often.

Bob: They started off having a competition that was run by the Snowy. Batlow won it. They cleaned up there, so this area decided to have a competition of their own and they brought this crew up.

There was Adelong, Gilmore, Bombally, Tumut Plains — they all had a team in and we did up this old tank and took it down. They sent Snowy's winning comp crew round to set up. I think Batlow ended up halving their time with this old thing!

We had expert chainsaw operators. Strong men. There was one comp where they had these logs and sprinklers we had to climb over and we had a pump and lengths of hose and I think there were just three men in a team. Well most of them had two men carrying this pump and one bloke stroking along with a hose, but we had Alan Hughes and he picked the two man pump up so that left the other two blokes just carrying the nozzle for the hose.

Jenny: He was with the electricity.

Bob: He was an electrician. It was a more or less combined rural fire and town brigade. I think Freddy and myself are the only remaining crew in Batlow. We decided that we had to get a tanker so we bought the old Blitz, and we spent months in the forestry workshop. We stripped it right down to the chassis and rebuilt it. We completely built it at forestry to our standard and then we cleaned up every competition. We ended up going down to Mt Beauty and we cleaned up all the comps all round and that big shield that's up on the wall, we won it four times I think. Our Blitz, they used to put it on the back of the truck and take it down. The first time they went down they got ribbed to hell for bringing this big thing down on the back of a truck until it went round the course!

The Future

Bob: For some reason or other Batlow has always been united. A lot of areas you find the neighbours don't get on real well and there is a lot of infighting in brigades. We've never had that. We have had very strong captains. I spent six years with the town brigade and when we moved out of town I decided to join the bush fire brigade as it was in those days. I went along to a meeting and they were looking for a president and they said all you have to do is chair a meeting. I don't know how many years… twenty years.

A Resilient Bunch

Janet Peel

Well, our story began on 30 December 2019. My brother Rob and his wife travelled up to Batlow on their motorbike as we were going to be heading to Merimbula the next day together on our motorbikes for New Year's Eve.

As that night progressed and we were watching news and listening to various reports it became very obvious that we weren't going to be going anywhere. My brother Rob and his wife packed up in early hours of the morning and made the journey back to Orange while they still could.

My husband Rodney was very busy over these next few days, out helping Steve our neighbour prepare all his property out at Kunama. They were in a race against time.

Things were very much starting to get very real and quite stressful. I didn't see much of Rodney over these days. He did get back to our house one day and advised me to pack up the car with treasures and valuables. My dad lives in town as well on the next street up from us. We are on Mayday Road and Dad is on Bartlett Street and his home backs onto the bush. I encouraged Dad to also pack up some valuables into his car.

There were town meetings being held in the Batlow RSL Club with RFS, Council, and Bushfire reps all there to fill us in on the predicament of our town and to answer any questions and concerns that people had. Those meetings were packed with Batlow people who were very, very worried about the dangerous situation. I left these meetings in tears as did many other people. The more serious things got the more higher-up in authority people come to address the townsfolk.

I evacuated out of town one night and drove to Tumut. I actually wasn't sure where I was going to stay, but was going to sort it out when I got there. I pulled up in Tumut and a work colleague phoned me and asked if I was okay and I told her I was in Tumut and needed a place to stay. Liz said to come straight around and she would look after me. Liz was so kind and hospitable to me that afternoon and evening. I got word that it was okay to go back to Batlow the next day so I drove back. My dad evacuated the same day as me to Tumut and stayed at our cousin's place and he came back to Batlow the next day also.

There was so much thick smoke all through the town and in our homes and lots of ash and embers floating around through the air. It was really, really awful.

My neighbour Chris Horsley and I were checking on each other as well. Our young neighbours Brad and Emily and two little kids had already evacuated to Tumut to her family.

I knew our top neighbours, Michelle and Leon, were away and their daughter Bree was home, so I checked on her too and she organised for a cousin to come and pick her up and take her to Tumut.

'We were told our town was undefendable. These were terrifying words to hear.'

I also checked on my Aunty Connie and her son. Aunty Connie was with her son Michael, his girlfriend and two grandsons which was good and they were heading out of town to hopefully find somewhere to camp near water.

Following the final town meeting we were all told in no uncertain terms to get out of Batlow as soon as possible while there was still a small window to do so!

We were told our town was undefendable! These were terrifying words to hear and a lot of people left the meeting that day very, very upset; me included.

I knew I couldn't leave Batlow unless I knew my dad was safely out too. He phoned my sister in Albury and arranged to go over there and I phoned my youngest son in Wagga and arranged to go there.

However in the meantime, some young teacher friends of mine who had just been married in October had all their very special things in the teacher flats including Ethan's pride and joy, a red Mustang car. This was really troubling me. I had a key to their unit so I contacted them in Wollongong and asked them if they wanted me to get some special things for them out of their unit and also to try to arrange for someone from Tumut to drive the Mustang down there. Vanessa Keenan and Sally Keenan's partner came up from Tumut and Vanessa drove the Mustang back to Tumut.

Bear in mind while all this was happening people were leaving Batlow in droves and in fact by the time we were up at Taylor and Ethan's unit, Batlow was like a ghost town. Taylor was able to text me precisely where everything valuable and their treasures were located — I was so amazed by this. I followed her instructions and everything was exactly where she said. I put in a few extra things too that weren't on the list.

Vanessa said to me 'are we all right to go?' and I said 'yes' and we pulled the front door shut and the very second I did this I looked at Vanessa in horror. She asked 'what's the matter?' and I told her I had just locked my car keys in the unit.

I was very heightened at this stage. She said to take a breath and asked about a spare set of car keys which Rodney had told me to put in my handbag the day before. That was locked in the car. We all were very upset at this point trying to think straight.

We thought about breaking the front door down, however there were reports of people looting and this would just leave it open slather! We checked every window and found that the kitchen window which was up pretty high and was reasonably narrow was open about a centimetre.

So I climbed up on Terry's shoulders and got it open and clambered through the window. I was relieved to get my car keys and for all of us to get out of town while we still could.

I drove out of town at 130 kilometres per hour that day. I was so heightened and stressed. The smoke was so thick also and was thick most of the way to Wagga.

Unfortunately, in my haste I took all the phone chargers and my husband didn't have one so his phone went flat and I lost some contact with him which was terrible.

The days leading up to Black Saturday, the 4th of January, were really hard and we were constantly listening to the news updates to see what we could find out.

Our daughter was overseas on holiday at the time and this was so hard on her being so far away and hearing all these terrifying stories about Batlow.

She was very close to jumping on a plane and coming home. We were able to encourage her that we were okay and for her to stay on her once in a lifetime trip.

The good thing with modern communication these days we were able to keep in touch and reassure each other.

On that Saturday I said to my son that I needed to find a church. Unfortunately the churches aren't open on Saturdays. However Braden's wife Emily suggested the chapel at Calvary Hospital.

I drove there and spoke to a lady at the desk and explained the situation and she let me go in. It is a beautiful little chapel and I got on my knees and started praying like I have never prayed before. Some dear Christian friends, Douglas and Berlinde Rand, phoned me while I was there. They evacuated to Sydney and we had some very powerful prayer together and their encouragement to me was overwhelming. There were a lot of tears that day.

My husband also managed to text me that day when I was in the chapel, not sure how he did with his phone going flat but it was so good to hear from him. He told me they would do their best to stay safe and that the fire was coming rapidly, and it was very bad. He told me he loved me very much and that now would be a good time to pray!

I stayed at the chapel for quite a long while, I played some music as well and prayed and cried to the Lord for his mercy and for his protection of our town and more importantly the few brave men who stayed behind to defend our town.

Later in that evening I got the best phone call and it was from someone who Rod works with and he phoned to say that Rod was okay and the town survived. I can hardly describe in words how relieved I was to receive that call.

Our town lost power and water supply wasn't safe to drink, no shops open etc. The Batlow Hotel stayed open through all of this. I am so grateful that Linda and Matt Rudd did this for the people who stayed behind. They gave the fire fighters somewhere to come for a meal and a cold beer and also some company. Rod was putting word through to us that there was very limited food and water etc and supplies. This was very troubling to us all.

Gareth is our daughter's partner and he lives in Albury. He was very affected by this event and the dire situation. He took it upon himself to go around to businesses and seek some donations and also purchased a lot out of his own pocket.

He obtained a large trailer and, with a mate's help, made his way to our little town with much needed supplies including ice, food and water. At this stage they weren't letting anyone into town; however Rodney was able to escort Gareth to Batlow with his work fire unit so Gareth got through. Yah!!

He had special packages made up for Rod and Steve as well and delivered them to our home. This meant the world to us and to a lot of people especially Rod and Steve. It was a very kind and brave gesture from Gareth.

Some power was slowly returning to Batlow but not on Mayday Road. Rod told me to not to hurry to come back until the power was back on and water was right too. I spent about a week and half in Wagga and then went across to Albury for a few days.

It was an extremely emotional drive back into Batlow for the first time! The devastation and loss was enormous. I had tears streaming down my face.

It has been a very hard and trying year for us but we are a resilient bunch and there was been a lot of healing that has taken place and regrowth and renewal happening which gives hope for the future.

I am pleased to say that my husband and I are now part of a group called Do It For Batlow that is working very hard towards the rebuilding and renewal of our town.

Sarah on Janet Peel

Janet is Batlow born and bred. A kind, warm and thoughtful woman, she loves her town and the people in it and wouldn't choose to live anywhere else.

She married a local man Rodney Peel in 1982 at the tender age of 19, Rodney was 20; and together they raised their three children in the town.

In Janet's words 'I'll do everything in my power to help Batlow and its community to thrive and blossom'.

And she does. If anyone is new to town and Janet is aware of it, they can expect a food delivery and a friendly welcome to *her* town. If you're in trouble Janet and Rod will be there offering help and support without being asked, delivering a load of wood, cooking a meal, or anything else they know will be of the greatest assistance.

Rubble and Ash

Brigid Bates

'This family home within the township of Batlow was reduced to rubble and ash on 4 January 2020, along with generations of family heirlooms, precious mementos from the childhoods of the parents and children and many irreplaceable keepsakes.

So many things would have been passed on for many more generations if it hadn't burned to the ground that day.'

The Greatest Victory   Phillip Quarmby

Apart from the occasional siren, the town was eerily quiet early on that Saturday afternoon. The battle was being fought on the outskirts of town by the RFS and local landowners. I was preparing my property whilst trying to get a little sleep to go back out on the truck that night.

Changeover never came, we were told the fire had jumped the containment lines, all crews were heading back to town and anyone waiting at the fire shed was to drive around town looking for spot overs. This period of anticipation was the worst feeling, not knowing what to expect and where to expect it from.

It was about this time, I had two members of a media crew approach me to inquire which was the best way out of town. The scared, hopeless and dejected looks on their faces when I explained that it was too late to leave, I will never forget.

I met up with my two brothers at the top of Cemetery Rd just in time to see one of the two main fronts come through. Watching the height and intensity of the firestorm, it was hard to fathom that anything would be left in its wake. To the east of us, spot fires had sprung up in paddocks and were rapidly flaring up.

As we went to work putting out flames around the family home, we could only watch as our paddocks and orchard burned. From the vantage point we had on the hill, we could see red glowing flames through the thick smoke at the top of town, gas bottles were exploding giving off the feel of a warzone.

Once things were contained up our road, we went into town to help where

we could. The number of spot fires in random yards was incredible. Some could be extinguished by stamping on, others could just be held at bay long enough in the hopes a tanker would arrive.

It was a tremendous relief as the night went on, seeing and meeting up with people we knew remained in town.

Getting through the day without loss of life was the greatest victory!

'Watching the height
and intensity of the firestorm,
it was hard to fathom that
anything would be left
in its wake.'

Not the Sunrise (Part I)

Michael Blenkins

Dunns Road

A lightning strike during a summer storm in late December 2019 brought our attention to the Ellerslie district. My family and I had driven past the nondescript Ellerslie Road signpost on countless occasions, and we had even driven up that long road to purchase hay in the 2000s.

But by the end of December 2019, the Ellerslie bushfire, which became titled the Dunns Road Fire by the RFS, was soon at the centre of our attention and thoughts in the Snowy Valleys Council.

News of the Dunns Road Fire captured our household's attention. We routinely monitored the RFS Fires Near Me site and its assortment of one-sentence updates and maps. I examined the map, and expressed concerns about the fire and its status. I recall saying to my family that I felt there was a potential problem on the cards if the fire managed to enter the plantations behind Tumblong, as the fire would possibly make its way up to Gundagai.

But as I studied the maps a little more closely, I speculated to my wife, Sulari, that *if* the winds drove the fire from the north-west, there might be a chance the fire could even get to the Green Hills pine plantations. And, if that were the case, then we'd be in real trouble at Batlow.

For decades we had kidded ourselves that the State Forestry would never allow a fire to damage the precious plantations of the region that were the cornerstone of local industries and employment. But the reality of economic rationalism (which was so popular and short-sighted when I was kid at university), and the reduction in State Forestry staff over the 2000s and 2010s, was a sobering reminder that local and corporate knowledge had been lost and never really replaced. Maintenance programs had been deemed 'inefficiencies' and vital plant and equipment had been sold, or its provision outsourced to the private sector.

The Forestry Workshop — perhaps the last jewel in the crown of State Forestry in Batlow — was decommissioned and now sat idle and empty. Thank goodness that Dunns Road fire was miles away.

My father in-law, Nihal, had been visiting us for Christmas and was due to depart by train for Melbourne with my son, Atticus, in the early hours of the morning from Wagga Wagga. After an early family meal, we set our alarm clocks for 11 pm and hit the road. Our trip to the Wagga Wagga Railway Station adhered to our cautious night-time driving ritual — drive no faster than 70 kms per hour — just in case Skippy or a wallaby decides to commit kamikaze on our car's grille. We drove to Adelong chatting, but the mood became rather awkward and ominous once we made our way between Adelong and the highway. To our left an eerie orange glow contrasted the darkness of night and defined the hills beyond Ellerslie Road. My father in-law commented on the remarkably early sunrise. But it was not the sunrise.

I disillusioned him.

He expressed amazement that the fire was still ablaze and that the authorities had not put it out with the aid of modern-day fire-fighting techniques, planes and so forth. Understandably, the remainder of the trip over to Wagga Wagga was awkward, as our thoughts now focused on the fire grounds we had passed.

I had told Sulari that I once I got home I would pack my RFS kit, as I expected a shift with a blacking out crew the next day. Farewells at the railway station's platform were brief as our minds were elsewhere. There was little discussion of the Christmas gathering, as we bid farewell to my youngest son, Atticus, who was accompanying his grandfather to Melbourne for a week. It turned out to be a bit longer than that.

The menacing glow of the fireground that night was perhaps the wakeup call we needed. Sure, we had a few annual bushfire precautions that we observed at our West Batlow farm: gutters were cleaned; water transfer pumps were tested; and the faded-red 1967 Bedford (a bargain $600 Ebay purchase, despite the absence of functioning brakes) was laden with 2,000 litres of water and a 5.5 HP pump (another Ebay purchase). A Chinese 'cheapo' generator was tested, and the unit was driven from our hay shed to be nestled behind the house.

My logic was that if we ever lost our power supply in a fire (which had happened one New Year's Day in the early 2000s), we could run at least two electric pumps with the generator. My wife and sons had reluctantly engaged in my practice drills once or twice — collectively displaying the interest of my least-engaged high school students — but the procedure was reassuring nonetheless. The process of using a combination of fuel, brute strength, generous sprays of Aerostart, and 'bad language' meant that we could hose down the house and verandahs if there was an ember attack.

Ellerslie

As I had suspected, the next morning I was called out with a black-out crew. These crews demand men (and women) of talent, energy and ability! Our crew consisted of Phil Withers, Cooper Smith and me. We were driven by our Brigade Captain, Darryl Watkins, to receive a briefing from a change-over crew near Wondalga. My memory of this is a bit of blur, but I think we swapped with a night crew consisting of Roger Watkins, Jeff Kynaston and Greg Walsh. The boys were tired as they had been on the fireground all night, but they possessed enough energy to stir Jeff who is the perpetual butt of Batlow RFS banter.

The journey to the mustering point was slow in our trusty Cat 3 Mitsubishi Canter laden with water. It was evident that the day was heating up and news of other fires ablaze across the state were being relayed through the media. We arrived at Ellerslie Road with dozens of RFS trucks representing small brigades throughout the area and some other units belonging to the private pine operators.

Official instructions were issued: our convoy followed a goat track that branched off the Ellerslie Road. My mind could see some humour — as the atmosphere reminded me of a *Dads Army* episode from my childhood. The instructions were complex and official, but also uncertain.

Prior to embarking on our patrol of the fire ground, we met and bantered with RFS members from Tumbarumba, including Frenchie and Jacob Shore (a former student), and brigades from the Tumut district. We were amazed by the place names (some unpronounceable) of different RFS trucks from villages, sidings and rural centres across the Riverina and South West Slopes. It was positive to see that the divisions that had characterised the unwilling marriage of the old Tumut and Tumbarumba Shires had been temporarily forgotten as we now faced a common enemy.

As predicted, by mid-morning the temperature was soaring. But on a positive note, the initial fire from the previous days appeared to have been contained. Flames were not visible; smouldering root systems and tree limbs were swiftly met with generous lashings of water. Phil observed that the pine trees in the plantation were pathetic in size and stature — and now they bore the added humiliation of being burnt. The blackened fireground was dangerous. We had been instructed to patrol and remain on the tracks that bordered the private forest and national park. Occasionally, we saw evidence of smoke emerging and we ran out hoses and used McLeod tools to rake out offending embers.

'CRACK'

When I was clearing around a smouldering tree's base, a large limb fell from above and missed me by only centimetres. In his typical good humour, Phil told me it had been my lucky day and that I should have been dead. He said it was time to buy a lottery ticket as I had only narrowly evaded a decent knock on the head. We rolled up the hoses and re-filled our truck's tank as our supply had dwindled.

I vividly recall copping a dressing down by a senior RFS official later for being over-enthusiastic and double checking the unburnt grasses in the powerline clearings.

The mini lecture included a curt reminder for us ill-disciplined Batlow RFS boys to 'sip' water to avoid dehydration on such a hot day. Collectively, Cooper, Phil and I felt like naughty school boys.

The heat intensified and wind speeds, as predicted, picked up around midday.

A scene that sticks forever

in my mind was the desolate, bright yellow summer-ravaged valley where the RFS crews assembled for lunch. The mood from earlier in the day had changed: it was now one of awkwardness and anticipation.

The farm houses near us appeared to have seen better days in the 1960s and 70s, but were now seemingly abandoned and unloved. A few trees offered precious shade as we tucked into sandwiches and bottled water. Kangaroos which had escaped the initial fire were not scared of the RFS teams and waded into dams to drink and cool off.

I was chatting to Phil and Cooper, when I suddenly felt that my eyes were playing tricks on me: the dark shadows cast by trucks and other vehicles in the midday sun seemed to be growing and moving. I soon realised that the black shadows were,

in fact, rapidly growing fires around us: little flame was actually visible; and at this time, no dramatic air-borne embers were apparent, but the ground around us was seeming to combust.

Lunches and conversation were abandoned. The menacing fires were stopped in their tracks with hoses and water. Blackened patches now contrasted the golden landscape hundreds of metres from the fireground we had been patrolling along Dunns Road.

Within minutes, radio messages on the UHFs became alarmed; hectic reports relayed how fires were randomly spotting miles away. Rather than re-trace our track along Ellerslie Road and back onto the Snowy Valleys Highway, we headed out to Yaven Creek via the Westbrook Road. Water tankers were relocated in haste. We joined RFS crews at two or three vantage points on properties along the Oberne Road trying to determine the fire's new locations and direction.

At one property which overlooked thick bushland to the West, I ran into the familiar faces of kids I'd taught at Tumbarumba High — Brad and David Nicholls — who were seasoned members of the RFS Humula Brigade. The afternoon heat intensified, the distant unleashed fire moved at a rate producing plumes of dense grey smoke. Air support was seemingly the only option to stop the bushfire and its multiple fronts, as it moved through the tinder dry and inaccessible bush.

The blackened fireground of Dunns Road at Ellerslie was no longer under control or 'being contained' to use RFS jargon — it was, in fact, a distant memory. The fire ground had moved in various directions and was indiscriminate. Fire coms reports were frantic — suggesting that the fire was escaping from the confines of the fire ground to search for fuel and destruction in all directions.

I remember reports of the fire jumping roads round Nakk Nakk and Adelong. Desperate calls were made of new sightings of smoke and fire. We moved along the Westbrook and Yaven Creek Roads into more familiar territory. Cooper commented that he was glad to see 'familiar vegetation' leaving the parched valley of charred and stunted pines.

We discovered that bad news travels fast — and met a line-up of watchful and tense farmers with slip-ons, including Geoff, Anthony and James Grady and Scotty Pearce. Over the UHF we heard updates and observations and requests for assistance being relayed by Andrew Scoullar.

The district was on fire, but we were not alone — as across the state, new fires were emerging as a combination of catastrophic conditions needed for a perfect firestorm unfolded.

I could not help but think that these were the very same conditions that a group of retired RFS and CFA commissioners had warned the Commonwealth Government about in their vain, well-intended lobbying efforts.

On the RFS website, the map of NSW was now barely recognisable — distorted by hundreds of red and yellow fire symbols which competed for space and relevance on a cluttered, overlaid map which charted the history of the fire season which we would call the Black Summer Bushfires.

Control Burns

The following days focused on coordinated control burn efforts around Batlow. My son, Edmund, and I were assigned to crew under the charge of Roger Watkins — or 'Mary' as he is better known by many. The humour and banter of the Cat 1 cabin was sarcastic and witty, not dissimilar to an episode of MASH. I felt strangely like Major Charles Winchester sharing a tent and operating theatre with Hawkeye Pierce and BJ Hunnicutt.

Roger had decades of fire-fighting experience, a vast knowledge of every geographical nook and cranny in the local area, and an ability to drive anything anywhere. Edmund had been away with RFS strike teams at the Grafton fires which had persisted earlier in the year. When Edmund started to drop the occasional expletive * [An expletive is a swear word, a curse you let out when you are startled or mad. The vocabulary website suggests these substitutes: fudge, sugar, heck and walrus. SourceVocabulary.com]. I felt, as a father, compelled to gently counsel him.

'That's enough of that inappropriate, bad language, Edmund!'

Roger whole-heartedly agreed; Roger looked at Edmund and sternly lent his voice in support. 'Listen to your father, boy! There is to be no more of that #@%!+# swearing. It's #@%!+# appalling, it's not #@%!+# good enough. Listen to your #@%!+# father.'

'I'm... sorry, Rodg.'

'That's better, boy. No more of that #@%!+# inappropriate language.'

The smirks on their faces revealed an alliance of rogues that would endure. I was now well and truly out of my depth outside the school yard with these two fellas! My suggestion of a swear jar for the duration of the fires was accepted but I don't recall any money being contributed to it in the following weeks.

Departure

By 29th December 2019 the fire had made its way to Willigobung where Edmund had fought a harrowing RFS shift alongside Roger and Greg Walsh. At the time, Edmund provided a desperate assessment to Sulari and me: homes and sheds had been lost at Willigobung, Laurel Hill and nearby Kunama. Some information was unclear, but it seemed the fire also had made its way along the Courabyra and Taradale Roads.

In the early hours of the morning, the police had called at our property Grand Oak on the Old Tumbarumba Road recommending we leave. This advice coincided with intermittent calls to my wife from Edmund—telling his mum to ignore *me*, and get the hell out of Old Tumbarumba Road, as the situation was hopeless.

I must admit I had thought disaster was imminent: the township of Batlow by now had been declared undefendable; and areas to the west, south and north of Batlow were deemed equally undefendable.

Edmund's dramatic advice from the firegrounds at Willigobung and Kunama to get out, and a police visit, went unheeded as we were determined to defend our home. However, the penny really dropped when our normally casual neighbour Ralph Winter called in to tell us he was leaving Illaroo, his family orchard. We then realised things were really desperate.

With a backdrop of smoke and wind, Ralph chatted to Sulari and me; he had his car loaded on his truck and was leaving for Tumut. We shook hands. I told him it had been great being neighbours for twenty-odd years — and that I hoped we might be neighbours again after the fires. I was being optimistic.

We started to relocate to a vacant rental property kindly made available to our family by our friends Albert, Carol and Carla Manning. We felt so grateful and very safe.

Our last night at Grand Oak, Sulari and I had sat upright in camping chairs, rather than risk sleeping. We sat in our house yard looking out

to the west. There was no need for lights as as the forest around the house was backlit with a red glow.

Sulari, aware that I had been on shift most of the day and was due to commence another shift the next morning, encouraged me to go to sleep. But I sat there determinedly all night, expecting an ember attack or something akin to what we had observed at Ellerslie a few days before. Nothing resulted. At some point I was convinced that I had heard the sound of an aeroplane flying about — and my mind immediately thought the cavalry had arrived to save us. I had images of Elvis (the water bomber) depositing its payload of water or fire retardant or a plane undertaking lask-minute reconnaissance on the fires to our west. This optimism was all wishful thinking on my part. There were no planes.

The sun rose on the 31st of December. Before it set again, we bid farewell to the house. We left it as ready as we were able. Crudely-fashioned nozzles sprayed the house down. Towels were soaked in water and pushed into doorways and window frames. We filled bathtubs, bathroom basins and sinks. Fuel containers were decanted and pumps filled. Of course, one of the 'good' firefighting pumps decided to die and we were forced to rely on a 4 HP motor (another Ebay purchase) and its antiquated belt-driven pump (a Gumtree bargain, perhaps better suited to a museum exhibition).

Sulari and I gathered a few tools (a hack saw, tenon saw and our forever unreliable multi-grips) and re-organised pumping fittings from our home's main water tanks. Hoses were positioned on our ridge capping, and our gutters were plugged with half bricks wrapped in wet tea towels. The generator was re-filled and set to run another two electric pumps spraying water over other parts of the house.

We look a few photographs with our mobile phones. The old Bedford truck sat looking unimpressed in the driveway next to the house — our final fire plan enacted (and obviously inadequate) — its lights and white grille resembled a face seemingly frowning at our cowardly departure.

The situation was hopeless; the hot winds were predicted to intensify in terms of their speed. Empty fuel containers and gas cylinders lined our front fence; gates were left wide open and the doors were not locked, just in case a team was nearby when the fire hit. Our lawn mower sat lonely and rather ridiculously in the middle of the parched yard. Out of habit, I was half-tempted to put it away in the shed, but this action or normalcy seemed futile at the time.

As we drove up the Old Tumbarumba Road we passed our immediate neighbours, the Browns and Steenholts, who were staying to defend their place. They had amassed an impressive assortment of vehicles and earthmoving equipment to sort out the fires on a military scale. Their equipment sat ready in the paddock adjoining their homes reminding me of the post-apocalyptic vehicles in the *Mad Max* films. They were ready for anything.

In the meantime, our poor old red Bedford sat back at Grand Oak, and our last supplies of water had wet down the house.

Until They Could Look After Themselves

Wayne Dubois (Transcribed from Oral Account)

We were trapped in Wagga, when we evacuated like we were told to. After a week of preparing my house, and both neighbours' houses on either side. We thought we were going to hang around but we couldn't. The next-door neighbour doesn't really live there, so she has blackberries this high. If her house caught fire, it was going to transfer to mine so I did my best to prepare it.

In Wagga grants were coming through for the farmers and others but nothing about the wildlife. Nothing at all for the wildlife. Nothing.

So I actually said to my other half, I'm going to help when we get back. I am going to put my hand up and help the Fireys, RFS or whoever is in charge of this thing.

Then driving up that hill for the first time we seen the devastation. So you felt obliged straight away. Well, I did any way. Once I was home, I literally unpacked and just got everything I knew would hold water. Every bucket that I had, every pot I had and I didn't have that many — to fill up with water to go out bush. Because the wildlife was going to need water.

We had a week of 40-plus degrees previous to the fire. Then after the fire — before people were let back — we still hadn't had any rain. And everything was burnt. I just knew they would need water. It was desperate.

I didn't have any food for the animals, so I went to IGA and bought a hundred dollars worth of groceries — just lettuces, carrots, broccoli.

I went out bush and then it just hit me. As soon as you get out there, there's just nothing, it's just total silence. It's just deafening silence — scarier than any horror movie.

I have thousands and thousands of videos, I've got trail cams I set up at feed stations just to monitor what was there, what was put there, how much food we should be putting there.

I've never done this before. It was all a learning curve. I thought, I'll go help kangaroos in this area. What do kangaroos eat? What don't they eat? What should I be doing? What shouldn't I be doing.

Try to help them and kill them in the process? Desperate and long days.

I had to work. I work on an orchard but as soon as I knocked off work I headed for the bush until it got dark. Once it got dark, home and then research. What I should and shouldn't be doing, trying to get donations, trying to get something, trying to get someone to get me some hay or something like that.

It's lucky I've got a social media account. Without the social media accounts I wouldn't have got anywhere. I would have had to do it all on my own. Because of the social media accounts I got a bit of support. Even though I only have fishing followers, they generally love the bush, it's part of the big scheme of things. One of my fans actually knew about ARC (Animal Rescue Cooperative) and he told them about me. They got on to me and within a week and a half, two weeks they started getting food up to me and I could drive over and pick it up.

Should I go over and get that stuff? That's a day I could be out in the bush helping animals; because no one else wants to go out into the bush.

That was the problem –people actually going out there. There was a small, very

small, number of people who wanted to go out there, but then they hit the barrier of, 'Oh its closed, you're not allowed to go out there'. Bullshit. Bullshit! That was just a perfect excuse for them to go, 'oh well, it's too hard, I'm not allowed to go out there'. I didn't even think that was the case. I just went out there and helped the animals because I knew they needed help, I didn't think that I would be 'allowed to' or 'not allowed to' or whatever.

It was just the politics involved – the shit I dealt with trying to do something, when I thought there were already people in place to help the wildlife. There wasn't, there still isn't, it was ridiculous.

I was about three weeks into it before the forestry people actually saw me hand feeding an echidna and wondered what I was doing.

'What are you doing here?'

'Saving the wildlife, no-one is actually doing it.'

Yeah so I just continued to do that. And then slowly and surely more and more donations were coming in. So every single day I'd go out with at least one ute load of hay, apples, fresh produce, whatever I could get. Coming into all these stores in town for left-over food scraps and stuff. Just everything I could possibly get out there. But the more I did, the more I wanted to do. When you look at the map, you just see how much, (330,000 hectares) was destroyed you know. I don't do things by halves, and it was doing my head in. Eventually I got myself settled down because I was trying to help everything and I felt overwhelmed. I finally got to the point where I thought, just look after what you can, and look after them properly. I'd say that there were about 40 stations that I was looking after and eventually it moved to way over 100, but the wildlife needed it.

People tried to tell you they all died. All these animals are all dead. It's amazing how many survived. The sad thing is, I hate to put a figure on this, but a vast chunk of the animals that survived died later, because there was no support. There was no food there, no water and I know for a fact that just my efforts meant tens of thousands of animals stayed alive. That is how many animals are out there, you know. I just could not get to some areas because of trees down, or the distance, or all the rest of it. I was emailing politicians left right and centre trying to organise aerial food drops in all the areas where no vehicles could reach. That was just wasted effort.

There was one drop somewhere down on the coast. That was organised by the mayor I think. I tried to do all this myself and I nearly had it done too — just working with people that flew over from Khancoban. If I could get the food down to them they'd happily drop it off. But then they'd have to get approval. What I was doing and trying to organise — it was just too much, so I just did what I could and I accepted that nothing else was going to get done which was really, really hard I can tell you.

We didn't have cute cuddly koalas.

If we had koalas here everyone would be down here helping for sure. But because we don't, nothing happened, but it is amazing how many animals did survive. It blows people's minds, but in saying that, the deer population literally got wiped out. Don't know if I should tell you the horrific side of things but there were valleys where you could see forty, fifty deer dead in the creek. They are in the creek and they're dead, they got burnt in the creek. You know they're intelligent enough to head down to water but even in the water they burnt to death. Absolutely horrible stuff.

The kangaroos, I didn't know this until my experiences, but kangaroos are really flighty. You can literally scare them to death; come up behind them and say boo and they'll have a heart attack and die. So the fire, they survive the fire but they have a heart attack and die from stress. So from Batlow to the Blowering foreshore – zero kangaroos. Yeah so definitely the deer and the kangaroo were wiped out for the most part, to the point where a lot of kangaroo were gone. And emus. They can't outrun a fire. In all the efforts with the wildlife I only saw one lot of two emus, and one lot of three emus

I know the bush from taking in fishermen, so I sort of knew where the creeks and stuff were and thought the wildlife wouldn't really need support in there, they'd still have water. So I knew where to focus my efforts. Well I didn't know, but I just assumed that the best approach would be the tops of hills. From the top of Snubba down to Gilmore Creek and down to Blowering its like ten kilometres or more. If an animal got injured or hurt on top of that hill it had no chance. But there is a lot of survivors in there and they don't have the ability to get down to water, and there is no rain or dew to get water that way. So I focussed my efforts up on that hill to start with and then every other hill from there on.

The first few times I went out — you just think — they're all dead, you know. But as soon as you put a feedstation down you start seeing all this life.

They just knew very quickly that I was the one coming to support them. They knew to stand back a bit, not stand too close to me, but not go too far. They'd sit and just watch me until I'd finished, and as soon as I'd start driving away, they'd come down.

Wallabies, wombats and possums were the main survivors. Wallabies — amazing. There are so many wallaby survivors, it's ridiculous to be honest. I think, I don't know for sure, but I believe the wombat holes are what saved the majority of the wildlife. And the wallabies are smart enough; and small enough.

Kangaroos are intelligent enough, they are maternal, they love their babies so they stuff their babies in these wombat holes and continue on themselves. The mother couldn't get in there. The problem was, mother and father are dead now and these little joeys had nowhere to go.

One of the most heartbreaking things I have ever seen, and you would never

believe it to this day, a wallaby had fostered six kangaroo joeys. I saw her over the course of these two weeks and these joeys are following her around non-stop. The humans weren't helping them so they were helping themselves.

I supported them when they needed support. But you are training them to rely on you, so I just looked for regrowth and that's how I knew I could stop. There's enough regrowth now, there's some water nearby. They can look after themselves.

Getting into politics and stuff. Six weeks after I had been doing this, WIRES (NSW Wildlife Information Rescue and Education Service) decided to turn up and puff their chests out. And, while I'd wanted them here, they gave me nothing but trouble. I had to keep on proving to them the animals were out there; why I needed them to bring me this food and stuff; giving them evidence and taking them out there, showing them.

They went and did this dodgy drone survey. I don't know if you have heard of it, took a drone out there over the top of my area, and tried to say that they only spotted like one possum. But animals are terrified of drones.

They should know better than that! But they used that to justify pulling out. No more support for you now! 'We've done a ground survey, there's no animals out there, there's enough regrowth, everyone stop helping right now, stop right now and take everything out.'

Well that alone poses problems: if you have been helping them non-stop and then suddenly stop. This is what we had to deal with.

Even the Forestry. Once the head forestry person come in to see me, they are like, 'We love what you are doing, I love what you are doing, you should be able to do it, but you have to get authority, you know'.

So I rang the big boys and I actually got their ok, but not on paper. So I am allowed out there but don't go putting anything on social media and stuff. It's Catch 22. If I don't put anything on social media, I don't get support.

Yeah, so it's a tough one. WIRES had given ARC a million dollars, so even though WIRES was fucking hopeless I couldn't say anything bad about them to anyone. But they need to be exposed for these things, so yes, lots of politics involved.

I don't give a shit you know, how the fire started, who's responsible. This is doable, just do what we've got to do — go out there every day. I know I am not letting all those animals die. I am out there every day, I know what is needed, so I had a bit of a rant on social media, and I got the Batlow community support which is good. They all knew that I would know better than anybody when I needed to stop and I wouldn't be doing it to pay the bills.

I am busy, I am flat out. I work three jobs; I love golf and fishing but I was out there. I gave up golf and fishing for 10 months pretty much, to focus. I didn't have the time. Three times I went golfing through that experience and I felt guilty! I felt bad, like I am having fun when I could be out there with more animals. I am slowly getting my mind around it. It completely changed me — definitely the way I think. I'm slowly getting back into hobbies again but at the time I couldn't do it. It just felt like – no you need to go through with it, you can do that later on. The wildlife needs you right now, every single day they need you out there, you know.

You can't just do it half-arsed. The best thing about WIRES coming is once they realised that everyone is actually making an effort, they put it all down onto a map so that we knew who had stations where. That was the most horrible thing of all because my stations alone were four times more than everyone else put together.

There was about six other people who made a bit of an effort, and they were all just on their own properties. They just put a station or two on the edge of their properties and didn't really go out of their way and get out into the bush. Part of it was because they weren't allowed. The other part was, they didn't really want to either.

'Oh, I can't help, not allowed to go out.' 'I'd be out there if I could too, you know, but...' I just found it was an easy excuse.

I'm not allowed to either, but I am out there, you know because they need you. I was happy to go to jail if I had to. These animals need a bloody support and no way anyone was going to tell me it was unsafe for starters, because I know that bush better than anyone. When they had the forestry people actually working in there afterwards, some of the people working there were kids, 19 years of age. And you're going to tell me its ok for them to go in there and work but I can't go in to help animals. I've been going out there for thirty years. I know that bush like the back of my hand. I've got all my chainsaw certificates, know all the dangers to look out for, and because I had that I think that's why forestry went 'alright, you can do it but be bloody careful'.

But requesting and asking and begging for permission to go in and help the wildlife, it did my head in. Really did my head in.

Eventually I started to get a lot of phone calls from people, from Wagga: 'I'll come up and help you for the day'. But it's not really helping me if they just jump in the car.

'I appreciate your offer,' I'd tell them, 'but if you just get your own stuff going out there, go to a new area and help some other animals would be great,'

There should be some mechanism in place, a group that comes in and says: 'Who wants to help the wildlife? This is how to do it.'

But there is nothing in place.

Even the dos and don'ts of setting up a station and all the rest of it. There is nothing. You can't find shit online. I made it up as I went along.

So for the long term, for future events I think we need a department, a division, a person or whatever. I don't think WIRES should have to run it, I don't think

donations should have to cover it, I think it should be a government thing. We're Australia for Christ sake. We are the most bushfire prone country in the world, there should be emergency wildlife plans.

A better setup would be for the government to have a go themselves. Why should a person come here and expect the townsfolk, after everything they have gone through, to go out there and do everything themselves. They should be organising aerial food drops and all the rest of it. Helicopters going over the top they can cover such a big area and it's less dangerous for the people.

The problem now is that Covid is the big issue so this has all been put aside. Nothing has been put in place or is going to be put in place for future fires.

Even dealing with WIRES was supposed to help, but they were nothing but trouble. They were a deterrent. They put out calls for locals to come down. Every local that came down to try to help just got scared away.

'Oh, you have to sign this to say you are doing it on your own risk.' You gotta sign this, you gotta sign that, it was too much for people.

One lady that did help, don't know her name, got in trouble.

'Oh you shouldn't be putting your bird seed there, it should be higher, it should be lower' — that sort of thing. She was making an effort, you know, but that is the sort of shit that people who actually want to help have got to deal with and that alone is too much. Just helping, you have no idea how emotional it is. That's just the emotional side. Physically, again, you are lugging bloody hay down the sides of burnt-out bloody cliffs.

Some people are just not physically capable. June and Jeff are legends, absolute legends. They wanted to come out and help but obviously they can't, too old and stuff, don't have the right vehicle, so the only way they can help me is by getting any old scraps from Coles, Woollies or whatever and bring them to me. So every week they were in Wagga, Tumut, they'd go and get scraps and, sweet potatoes and they'd cut them up for me as well. They really wanted to help and that was the only way they could. It saved me going and chasing food, saved me cutting up. They were actually helping me, you know. There were so many times I just broke down, or wanted to break down. They'd say the right things these beautiful people.

Like I said the support was limited, very few people actually put their hand up, and the few that did they were deterred. No one helped. I put the map up and I did a 10-minute video of me talking about it and you can hear how emotional I am about the lack of support.

I've got a hundred feed stations but it is like a few little dots on the map. No-one is here, no-one's in here, no-one's doing anything through here, all these animals are starving. I know the wildlife is in there, alive, but they are just slowly dying without that support. Hitting every politician up. Joe McGirr he was the one who did, tried the most. Still got no-where for me but he had a crack for me.

There was no support. I tried every sort of grant you could possibly get but because I'm not in any organisation.

Seventy-six million dollars went to WIRES. By the time I'd pulled out and the wildlife didn't need any more help, they had spent six or seven million of that 76 million dollars. That wasn't in this area either.

I had so many enquiries from people asking where should we send money and I'd say, 'go to WIRES' — until I found out the facts. ARC are the only people who give 100 percent, it all goes straight back in where it should. They are really upfront with their expenditures whatever has gone in, this is what we spent it on.

ARC they are absolute legends. It's grown exponentially; it was like ten people and I was dealing with the guys who ran it. It was really stressful for them too.

That's one thing about WIRES that makes no sense. Why are the CEOs and the rest of it working in the office getting paid a wage, yet people like me, people down here that are in the field, have to volunteer. If anyone is getting paid it should be people who are making the difference, you know.

Like the RFS being volunteer. We've accepted this as a country and it's wrong. There should be a government organisation for this that's paying for it. We shouldn't have to donate and then see what WIRES decides to allocate here, there and everywhere. The whole system is bullshit. Absolute bullshit.

These are the organisations that are supposed to be there to help these animals and that's what they're doing, so what hope is there? It was a massive eye opener.

Recovery has been awesome.

Small birds are still there, not in numbers but pockets here and there. They'll come back quickly enough and it's surprising, actually, they started breeding straight away.

I saw little joeys poking their heads out at the food stations. Is it because of me that they are having their babies? They know they have food.

I seriously think another year or so and it is going to be exactly the way it used to be, with wildlife. The bush itself, 15 years or more before we get anywhere near what it used to be.

Wombats everywhere now. Nearly all the wombats survived the fires, no problems at all. It's just they starved to death afterwards. And it's horrible. I can't think of anything worse as a way to die. Nothing to eat within cooee. Not even

water. We actually put extra water stations beside dams because some of the forestry dams were black: the water was black. Every time it rained it got blacker and blacker. If this is their only water supply, they are going to die.

Fish have recovered big time. Definitely affected the trout a little bit, I'd thought they'd actually been wiped out, but no they moved into little pockets here and there and slowly moved back once we got the rain. We're lucky because everything drains out in the mountains, and washes real quick and it isn't there for too long. So the water flushed through, the trout survived.

But down on the flat country, once it got down to flat land like Adelong Creek, Adelong township, it's just flat land. Slow moving. No oxygen. All the fish died through there. Same as the Upper Murray before it gets into Lake Hume. It's pretty flat down there as well, those dry creeks beds filled with ash and then we had rain, the rain washed all this ash in, the cod, yellow belly, carp, even platypus — everything died. But only in a 10 km stretch. Once it got into Lake Hume it filtered out.

I was out in a pine forest, in a tiny little pocket along the creek and there were little dams there, but it was all burnt out around. There were platypus alive in these little dams. No-one knows what to feed a platypus. I was getting on to all these websites and couldn't find anything! What are they going to eat?

I had a station 20 metres or so away from the dam, for the wildlife and stuff. But I was feeding kangaroo pellets and vegetables and that. Still, I started seeing scrape marks coming out of the dam over to the feed station — on the other side of the road. I've only seen footage of platypus eating yabbies and that sort of thing, but I suppose a desperate animal with eat anything. I was worried I was going to get the bloody platypus killed, so I moved the station away from the dam.

Sulari on Wayne Dubois

Wayne has lived in Batlow for more than 35 years since his family first moved here when he was a young child.

Best known as his fishing persona 'Mr Freshwater', Wayne proudly promotes Batlow and the surrounding bush via his social media, and articles in Australia's biggest fishing magazine publications, as well as monthly reports on fishing options, putting Batlow on the map as an outdoor destination with fishermen, hikers and campers alike.

He has worked on and managed apple orchards for the last 20 years and is a successful member of the local golf club. Always a champion of the Australian bush, his love of our native animals drove his extraordinary response in the aftermath of the fires.

I'll Never Lose That View   Anne Hallard

'There's a fire evacuation order for Batlow. A town hall meeting has been called at the Batlow Literary Institute. Tonight at 8 pm. I've advised the incoming guests.'

These were the stark words I heard from Brindabella's housekeeper, Glenda, as I travelled back home from a Christmas break in Queensland.

My mind racing: how has this happened? Where is the fire coming from? When and where did it start? How could it have escalated to the point of evacuation so quickly?

I drove through the night to the farm with my son Andrew. The 'Fires near us App' became a symbol of how reliant we were on understanding our new unfolding world.

'Mum this fire is travelling faster than we're driving', was my son's comment that

made us both realise we didn't know what to expect when we arrived at our farm, Brindabella Farmstay.

The ensuing five days consisted of a combination of negotiation, disorganised organisation, fraught decision making, information processing — all the while trying to remain positive that the situation wouldn't transpire as predicted.

Central to my concerns was Angela, the bride who had booked her wedding to be held at Brindabella the following week. Having spent a lot of time staying at Brindabella with her family to organise the wedding the previous year, I was paralysed with the 'what if' scenarios I may need to discuss with her.

After final evacuation orders were issued, Andrew and I left the farm. We stopped at the front entrance and I glanced back, as I heard Andrew's words, 'this is everything you've worked for Mum'

The phone call at 8.30 am on the morning of Sunday 5 January, after the fires the night before, was as difficult for Tom, a family friend who had stayed to fight the fires in Batlow the night before, as it was for me.

'The house is gone Annie, but the shed and glamping tents have survived'.

I was fortunate to be allowed to visit the farm later that morning but the magnitude of devastation as we drove up the 'gap' from Tumut was indescribable.

I felt disorientated, unable to recognise familiar landmarks. Trees were smouldering, stumps burning, sheep lay where they had fallen and exploded. Driving down toward the house past the shed and tents was surreal.

As I walked around the smouldering remains of beautiful Brindabella Farmstay, I was completely numb. I had no words, no tears – just memories.

Finally as we left, I said 'well I've lost the house but I will never lose that view'.

As the days and weeks post-fire unfolded,

the outpouring of love and support from friends, family, voices from the past, guests of Brindabella and the whole town of Batlow was so incredibly overwhelming, I felt a commitment to 'dig deep'.

One dear friend Robyn rang to say she and her partner Dan had transferred $1,000 directly into my account in the hope it would help. That was the 'turn-key' moment that I decided I needed to 'get into gear' and start at the very beginning, by rebuilding the front gate with those funds. This rebuild was done with the help of Steve, Tony and Andrew who all worked to buy, cut and rebuild the gate. This was the new entrance to the new beginning.

Among the many emails and calls I received from guests of Brindabella was a mother who called me on behalf of her seven-year-old daughter Grace. The family had enjoyed a very memorable holiday at Brindabella some years prior. Since that holiday Grace had talked every day about wanting to have a farm in the Snowy Mountains just like Brindabella. So moved was Grace by what she saw and enjoyed at Brindabella, she painted her memories of Brindabella Farmstay as a gift to me. This I decided would take pride of place in Brindabella!

As this new beginning started to take place I reflected on the words of Catherine DeVrye (2005):

'Although we can't always control events in our lives, we can always control how we react to those events. It is our choice alone whether we adopt a positive or negative attitude in the face of adversity – to be victims or victors of those potholes in the road. If we approach bleak situations with a lightness of heart and spirit, stumbling blocks can become stepping stones'.

The glamping tents that still stand to this day have become symbolic of my determination to ensure Brindabella II is indeed a 'stepping stone' for the fourth generation of Hallards in Batlow.

Sarah on Anne Hallard

Anne is a proud third generation Batlow resident. She spent a very happy childhood on her parents' orchard 'Brentwood' on the Batlow Road. Childhood days were spent riding the steam train from Batlow to Tumut, riding her fixed wheel bike or her very temperamental horse Priscilla and helping out in the orchard. Her favourite time of year was cherry season when Ann would help pack cherries into wooden boxes for delivery around Australia.

Her parents sold Brentwood in 1980 and Anne moved to Sydney to work but her love of Batlow never waned. In 2006 Anne returned and purchased a small farm not far from Brentwood. Deciding that her love of Batlow should be shared, Anne commenced operation of Brindabella Farmstay.

Anne is a warm, engaging woman, and it is easy to see glimpses of the little girl who was undoubtedly happy-go-lucky but determined. She has that undefinable county-woman air of someone comfortable in their own skin; strength and competence combined with an understated style.

It wasn't much, but it was home

Michelle Wainwright (Transcribed from an interview)

We were in Port Douglas for Christmas. We heard about the fires but they'd started a way away, so we just continued our lives there. We just played golf, like we do every day, but then as it got closer, we lived by the radio. Like everyone did, so we could hear it. Our son, Andrew, was at home; our daughter, Sarah, was at Mum and Dad's in Tumut.

My biggest concern was that Andrew would want to stay and wouldn't know how to… We had no firefighting equipment.

So I said to my sister, Jenny 'Just promise me you'll get him out'. And she did.

I'm just trying to remember dates. So, we're living up there and still playing golf every day and being up there it was quite surreal. All of this is happening down here and we're hearing it, but when it hit, we… I think the hardest part was not knowing what was happening.

Brad, my husband, knows lots of people, but they still couldn't tell us, and we didn't expect them to tell us because they were there fighting the fire.

Andrew didn't leave until the last moment. Jenny saw fire in the trees and Andrew heard it come up the valley and that's when she said: 'We've got to go, we can't fight this. We don't have the equipment.'

That's when they left. And, I don't know, I can't even remember what day that was. I wouldn't have a clue.

We knew the fire had gone through Kunama on New Year's Eve. We thought we'd get on a flight, but QANTAS wanted to charge us, like, $4000 each. We got Brad on a flight on what must have been the 4th.

I got a phone call at the airport, and… and that's when I was told the house was gone.

And I couldn't contact Brad, because he was on the plane. The only person I could ring was my mum, and Brad's mum, because of course they're both mums.

So, I'm in port Douglas by myself because I had to go back and clean the house up. I wasn't on a flight until the 8th.

The drive from Wagga airport to Tumut was horrific. That was when highway patrol were still there and blocking off roads. It was very surreal. We were swimming in a pool and listening to the radio when all this was happening, not

knowing but what can you do? We couldn't go anywhere. As long as Andrew and Sarah and everybody was safe, that was my main concern.

It's a terrible feeling, because you're helpless, you can't do anything. Your loved ones are in Batlow, and they're fighting the fires and you don't know how they are. It's just trauma all round.

We listened to the comms. It was on all the time. We just listened to it, so much, that at one point the next-door neighbour got quite abusive at us to turn it off. Yeah. It wasn't on especially loud or anything, but it was on at night. I do understand night after night. But later someone told him what had happened. That's what it came to, it ruled your life. That was the only connection and you needed that, because you didn't know what was happening up here.

Tell us about the house

That's hard. It's hard because that was our life. We'd lived there for 25 years. We were a newly married couple, we moved here, and we had our babies here. It was an old soldier's settlement house – and it was home. You know, it had uneven floors, it had… It was beautiful, it had beautiful trees and gardens and you know that it didn't matter that it was tiny and it wasn't much, it was home.

I think that's what the kids have found hard: it was their home; they came home to it. Everything was in that house, it's all they've ever known. It was us.

And then you drive up the driveway and it's just this melted bit of tin on the ground and there's nothing. You have your memories in your brain but…

The fire pit and the pizza oven were still standing, and that was it.

Andrew couldn't leave. He never left; it was too hard for him. The police checked on him every day. But it's a loss, and you'll never get that back. I think the hardest thing was, and it's taken this long for me to realise this, that it wasn't our choice. It wasn't our choice to lose our home, we've built a new place but it's not home.

The new place is beautiful but it's not home. The old house contained everything we did in our lives before we got married, everything from when I went overseas — even the Waterford Crystal, which we didn't really use, but now it's just a melted puddle.

It's taught us to look at things differently, we look at life differently and we've reassessed. We're very minimal now and there's nothing much in the new place. We'll make new memories but lost so much. We've lost our wedding photos

I worked out the other day: We've lost the connection to that land; we've lost that connection we made over 25 years. It's just not there anymore. Will that take another 25 years to build?

We don't want to give another 25 years. That's the realisation we've come to. I look out the window and it makes me feel tired, because there's no grass and there's no trees and it's hard work. Maybe if I was 25 again, I could put that work in.

I still have my memories. Once the grass grows and the red mud's gone it'll be... It's exhausting.

Once the spring comes and there's grass, it'll be beautiful and the daffodils are coming up things like that, re-emerging, they're bright and cheery.

You have to get up, you have to move forward and that's what we've done. We had to design a new house, and that's what we've done. We've done it in a haze, and I believe we've done quite well but we really just had to get it done. There was no time but it does make you reassess what the future holds and maybe it's just brought forward our plans.

As principal of Batlow Technology School

I think having my job was another saving grace because I had to go to school and be a principal and look after the kids and the community. And you just do it.

I've seen some families fracture, some I would never have believed would fracture. And some have lost their homes. But also the kids, they're on edge. They haven't lost that yet, and I think it's a time thing. We need to be talking to them and letting them know it's okay to be sad on some days; and have those moments when they remember they lost their pony. They're on edge, all the time and it's changed the kids.

When they had to go, they worried about it, they worried about their homes. No matter what kind of home it was, it was their home; their place to go back to. We were fortunate that the school is in one piece, because if the school had been burnt, then how do we hold them together?

But I watch these kids, and they are more compassionate now. Any new student who comes into the school, they accept them, there's no judgement, they'll talk about the fires, and it takes a little bit to draw it out of them, but they'll tell the new kids about the fire and what they went through and if they lost something or how many times they were moved.

Before this, there were a lot of people who wouldn't have come to a meeting to support others. I see in the school community, parents being more open to their children seeing the counsellor which didn't happen before the fires. There was never that acceptance before, but now if I ring a parent, they'll sign the form. They're happy for their child.

I say, you can come too, and they're open to that. It's made them realise our kids do suffer inside and they do feel that stress. Especially when they were told the town's going to burn and we couldn't save it. Parents went into that mode of we have to look after our children, but how do we do that, we weren't ready for this.

The first impulse is to send the kids away, but they need to go together, they need their parents otherwise they worry. We do a lot more team building, and mental health activities, a lot more. We focus on that.

The Garden

We've got more trees falling down now. I wouldn't let them chop certain trees down, but I'm looking at them now thinking they're not going to survive. The bulbs, and everything like that are coming back. We're not allowed to plant within a 30 m radius of the house. It's a fire regulation. We could have replanted within that perimeter but that would have upped our fire risk and added about another $400,000 onto the cost of our build. It's a massive distance. We can plant shrubs and little things. I'm going to put olive trees in, not close to the house but around the water tank and down the driveway. I've got the one garden behind the pizza

oven which wasn't hit either – it went either side – and it's coming up. The backyard's just grass, well mud, but it will be grass. And no, I'm not planting any trees. Because I look at it, and I know it's probably cynical, but I know I'm never going to see them. I know it's for the future, and I get that, but we haven't even got rid of the piles yet. We still have piles of burnt trees.

We need to burn them before we can even think about growing grass and replanting. And we've got a massive burnt pile where the house used to be, it's still there. And one over near the common fence and one down the back near the house. It was just pushed into piles. The house debris went, this is just the trees.

In the ashes

I went to my bedroom, and I found a little jewellery box that Mum had given to me. It was metal, and it was full of melted jewellery. Andrew pulled a couple of things out. I had a champagne bucket that I'd bought in France, and he found that for me, intact. But Mum's things, not that they were valuable, just sentimental value, it was just one big, melted lump. I did keep it, but I haven't now. It was just too hard and decided I'm just not keeping it. And that's all we found. Oh, and one coffee cup. I didn't keep that either.

I now have matching coffee cups! Everything matches. That's why it doesn't feel like home. And it's not home. I've got a dedicated laundry! I didn't have a laundry as such in the old place. Everything works now! No dripping taps.

And I now have a garage and the door goes up and I drive straight in from the rain and the snow; and it only has my car in it. Everyone else has to park outside and I can get in from inside the garage. And I have a pantry.

It is lovely but it would have been nice to do it because we chose to do it, with our memories, and the things that make you feel at home. But anyway, I'm trying to get there, I've started baking and...

The hardest part, in a way, is the lack of clutter. We were trying to repair some polypipe lines and Brad said, 'Can you just go the shed and get a joiner,' and then he'd just look at me. Those tools he'd lost, and all the bits, the things he only used once a year or less, but knew they were there.

But look, there's still a garden and there's still a fire pit and the pizza oven. There will be a new fire pit behind the new house. Dual fire pits, a his and hers fire pit. I'm looking up beautiful designs and we've found a spot. It's good to live through a winter to see grassy area is currently grass which isn't any good in winter so we'll get it paved and make that our entertaining area.

So many things are different now: water pools in different places, the winds are different because so many trees are gone; it's colder, it's windier. We didn't feel the wind before, we were sheltered, but now the wind comes from everywhere.

My Sarah, who is very sentimental, rang all our family members and just said you need to copy any photos you have of us, our family, us as babies, of Mum and Dad and she got all these pictures and she made a beautiful album of them all. It's an interesting collection! And that's something for them to have as well. It's a very thick folder and it's full of every photo we ever sent or gave them.

And I did find our wedding negatives in the safe, but they're in their slips and one side is slightly melted onto the negatives. If I hold them up, I can see the pictures, so I need to find somebody who knows what they're doing; I want the whole lot printed again.

You know what I have in my wallet? I have the little, tiny photos of when the kids started kindergarten! I also have two framed photos, because Andrew asked me what I wanted out of the house and I didn't know what to save, so he just grabbed things. I had a bag with jewellery that Brad had bought me on occasions, and I knew where that was. And he picked up two of our wedding photos. He did very well, especially given the state he was in.

I think he feels responsible for not saving the house and not getting more stuff out. He feels that on his shoulders. And I just say: 'We wanted you alive, that's what was important.'

And if you can only pack ONE plastic tub, what do you take? What do you put in it? We do make strange decisions.

I was up carting firewood the other day, and there are still some trees with that very green epicormic growth. I can look at it think it's beautiful, but you know why it's there.

Like Another Planet   Darryl Thorpe

Initially, the smoke was not too bad, but it was very hard to know which direction it was coming from. I remember coming back home from a neighbour's house on Friday 3 January and seeing a highway patrol officer sitting in his police car, watching me casually mowing the lawns around my house. I didn't know what he was thinking, but something told me I had to mow the lawns very short to create a fire break around the house and garage.

I noticed that there was a 'voluntary evacuation notice' put on my door by the police. However, as I had already decided to 'stay and defend' and instigate my RFS bush fire survival plan (even if it was just in my head), I kept saying to myself, 'they can't throw me out'.

The fire pump was fuelled and ready to go, the transfer pump (on the creek) was fuelled and ready to go; and I had already blocked my downpipes and filled the gutters with water as recommended by the authorities.

I had my favourite, recently-restored 1944 army jeep parked in the woodshed. I realised I'd better move it, as the woodshed was full of firewood and would go up for sure. But where could I move it to? The garage was already full, with my two restored historic motorcycles and my new ride-on mower.

I kept looking at the RFS fire map and saw that the fire front was approaching from the south-west, so I decided to park the jeep on the eastern side of the house. Now the jeep has an oiled canvas roof, so I did not really expect it to survive. But I covered it with a plastic cover and put corrugated iron over all the seats, which were also covered in oiled canvas, to give it some more protection. A plastic cover? What was I thinking – doesn't plastic burn fairly easily?

Saturday morning 4 Januar — I went over my survival plan once again when a local RFS member checked in to see if I was staying to defend. I said 'yes'. However as the morning unfolded, another crew of RFS volunteers arrived and told me I'd better leave now, as conditions had deteriorated.

I remember reluctantly driving by the local fire shed and seeing lots of volunteers grouped up ready to go to work and had a sense of guilt that I was not able to help.

Looking back at the fire storm from the Gocup Road was surreal, as my mind was conflicted between staying to defend and being evacuated against my will.

Who was going to defend my house? That was supposed to be my job.

And I didn't want to go, so driving to Tumut was hard. My friends were not home and I had a sinking feeling of dread as I decided to drive to Cootamundra to another friend's house.

My friends were glad to see me and were keenly watching events unfold on the television. I stayed a week and another good neighbour (Trudy) who was also evacuated, kept me informed of events.

The week after the firestorm first hit seemed to drag out. Each day was agony, sitting in someone else's house, not knowing what I was going back to. When I was eventually told I could return, no one knew the extent of damage.

Driving back into the fire-damaged area was like being on another planet. All of the familiar things that humans take for granted were gone.

I felt a rush of mixed emotions when I saw my neighbour's house gone, but mine was still standing; including the garage and historic motorcycles. What about my favourite jeep?

That's when I first experienced 'survivor guilt'. Why was my wooden-clad house still standing and my neighbour's house gone?

And the smell of death (dead animals), lack of any animal sounds, no colour anywhere (black is not a colour) and the seemingly endless destruction, was an assault on my senses.

Even though I was allowed to return, I was not prepared for the psychological impact of the next week or so. I was wandering around in shock with my shirt off when some friends checked up on me. They found me just babbling on; no doubt it was delayed shock.

Part of the shock was that the army jeep was still standing! The firestorm and embers must have jumped over the roof; and the house shielded it from the intense radiated heat. Oddly enough, the plastic cover must have taken the heat out of the embers, as it was peppered with holes! One large ember did make it all the way through the plastic cover, then also the canvas roof, before it went out. The hole is still in the roof till today!

The intense heat had bubbled the paint on my garage doors and some of the plastic down pipes on the house and garage were melted; and everything else outside of the house and garage was destroyed. Every living plant, the woodshed (and all its contents), an old camper van, trailer, farm bike and all the fences were just gone.

There were coloured patches on the black grass where objects were 'vaporised'. I can't even remember all of the items that were there. I walked down to the creek and just saw a barren flow of 'black soup'. One day I noticed that there was even a dead 'cooked' trout lying on the bottom. The chooks had 'smoked fish' for tea.

No words can describe the total destruction. Everything was carbon black, it got onto all my clothes and the smell wouldn't go away. Amazingly enough, even though both the house and garage were locked up, a layer of ash made its way under the cracks in the doors and was literally piled up against the carpet tassels.

I then realised how close I came to losing everything.

One day I decided to ride around on my historic army sidecar to my neighbour's places to see if anyone needed a delivery of bottled water (which was donated) as I knew that my tank water was tainted with contaminates from the bushfire and possibly so was theirs.

Dealing with the initial impact of the fire was hard enough, but not as hard as what was to follow. People from various government departments just turned up at random. There were no communications as the telephone cable was totally destroyed in the fire.

Obviously, each department had a job to do, but none seemed to liaise with any other and I was caught up in the middle, forced to deal with people immediately after a traumatic event. This was very hard for me and the lack of understanding in general regarding this issue still disturbs me.

A small group of volunteers delivered me some food parcels which was very kind of them. What impressed me was their age; all young people who were willing to help a stranger. I went up to the trauma recovery centre in Batlow for advice from Legal Aid, as my insurance company was disputing my claim (which only exacerbated my distress).

I lost around three years' worth of cut firewood, which apparently was not covered by my policy, even though firewood is not listed as an 'exclusion'. I asked for some 'stock feed' for my chickens which was denied. However, a few days later those same young people brought me a few bags of feed.

I was amazed that some of the older folk at the recovery centre cast a value judgment that my chickens were not considered worth feeding (remember, there was not a blade of grass anywhere) yet people were walking out of the recovery centre with boxes of (donated) food. I only wanted some stale bread!

Blaze Aid were very helpful to me to restore the boundary fences, however the government appointed arborists came after the fencers and were felling trees on the new fence lines! Eighteen months later, the local contractors are still working to remove damaged trees and fences, which only prolongs the healing process (for me anyway, and I imagine some of my neighbours as well). I know of another neighbour who is still waiting for her shed to be re-built.

Of course everyone in the local area is in the same boat, still having to deal with contractors so long after the event. People can't 'move on' with their lives if too many issues are still unresolved.

My neighbour Trudy is now selling up and moving; and she is not the first one I know about to do this. I have and always will have, complete empathy for trauma survivors and the bushfires have only just reinforced this belief.

Sulari on Darryl Thorpe

I first met Darryl the day we returned home. Power had not yet been restored to Old Tumbarumba Road but we were just happy to be home, to begin cleaning up the mess. It was warm. We'd been clearing in the soot and the heat, and so we'd become acutely aware that there was also no water.

There weren't many vehicles traversing Old Tumba Road as only residents were being allowed back, and so we looked up when we heard the motor.

A WWII motorcycle complete with sidecar puttered up the hill. It stopped at our gate and Darryl removed his helmet and asked us if we'd like some water. He pulled several bottles from the sidecar and introduced himself.

Since then, we've come to know Darryl as a kind, gentle and sensitive man with a strong sense of right and wrong. He looks out for his neighbours, delivering unexpected kindnesses on antique vehicles.

Heroes!

Cheryl Crouch

Early morning smoke filled air
A nervous tension mounting
Anticipate of what's yet to come
Of wild-eyed terror and shouting

A thousand feet took up the beat
Our yellow army rises
For each one knew their duty
And prepared for no surprises

The captain called his soldiers
Said you may fight or may decline
Out of all his trusty volunteers
Not one man crossed the line

This will be a mighty battle
We may lose it in the end
But fight we will, my comrades
For our family, homes and friends

With the town evacuated
Only fighters stood their ground
To defend the undefendable
Was the rumour going around

As day turned into midnight
The earth shuddered under foot
The Captain gave his orders
And each one was undertook

With the roar of a mighty freight train
The monster charged up every hill
Nothing seemed to stop it
Its intention was to kill

The army sprang to action
And they fought it tooth and nail
If we can cut his bloody head off mates
We've got him by the tail

The heat and ash and embers
This monster was a freak
I fear we may have lost it boys
If it jumps across the creek

The fire raced on relentless
And the firies courage strong
The Captain called for air assist
Denied – smoke and wind is just too strong

The radio, trucks and fire
All made a mighty din
With both sides of the battle
Determined now to win

You'll not take our town you bastard
We'll fight you to the end
The fire hissed and crackled
As it swept around the bend

But fires can change direction
As they've oft been known to do
And this one did that very thing
That very afternoon

It missed the town and raced away
That brought the town reprieve
A thousand weary fireys paused
And fell down to their knees

Some say a hero wears a cape
And is an all-round friendly fellow
But in my eyes my heroes are
The ones all dressed in yellow!

Thank you. May god Bless You All!

Sarah on Cheryl Crouch

Cheryl moved to the area as a child with her parents. She recalls a 'large new house' in the Greenhills Forestry Camp which, on later reflection, was actually a small cottage which had to house their family of eight!

Cheryl completed her schooling in Batlow before moving away. She met her husband 'Blue' in Sydney, they married in Batlow and once he finished his time in the army they moved their four children 'back home'.

Blue is in the RFS but they were out of town during the fire and had to listen to the unfolding drama from afar.

When All Seemed Lost

Chris Horsley

There was more than one warning by night and by day,
With temperatures soaring and fire on the way;
With wind strength increasing and temperatures high
The message was simple. 'Get out or die'.

So 'get out' I did with an overnight bag,
A photo, an invoice and a feeling of sad;
Left town in a hurry, before roads were blocked;
Anxious, lonely, nervous and shocked.

I'm eternally grateful for the warnings that came
That the bushland near Batlow could burst into flame.
Having left before trees burnt from roots through to crown,
I didn't see disaster as it spread through the town.

I also didn't see what I believe to be true,
That the people who stayed seemed to know what to do.
They found water and vehicles and made it their task
To protect the 'undefendable' without being asked.

My hubby and his mate are among those I cheer
For saving my house and the things I hold dear.
They carry on now as if nothing was wrong
Demonstrating traits that make communities strong.

All shun the word 'hero' as they get back to normal,
But 'thank you' or 'cheers' just seems too informal
To acknowledge the character of Batlow's defenders
Who fought the fire that Batlow remembers.

Sulari on Chris Horsley

Several years ago Batlow hosted a crime writers' festival. *Murder in the Mountains* brought both writers and readers to our little town in the foothills of the Snowy.

As part of the festival theme it was proposed that crime scenes be created around town and its surrounds. That job was given to Chris Horsley who created a dozen detailed and whimsical crime scenes which not only told stories but were so realistic that we had visits from the police. Further she persuaded local business to get in on the act, and soon Batlow was rivalling Midsommer.

I speak of this as an illustration of who Chris Horsley is: community minded and clever, Chris has a well-earned reputation for getting things done. She has a mad love of costume and can create just about anything, including a sensation.

Chris and her husband Steve have lived in Batlow for over quarter of a century and have raised a son and a daughter in our town. Chris was the backbone of both the Apple Blossom Festival and Ciderfest and remains one of those energetic, talented and generous people that various local initiatives rely upon for help.

'Fire Comm – Fire Comm – Batlow Captain – Over'

Diana Droscher

'Batlow Captain – This is Fire Comm – Send – Over'

Those are words I don't need to hear again.

From August 2019 most of NSW was on fire and it just got worse from then on. My husband Brian and I are active members of the Rural Fire Service. We both belong to the Batlow Brigade, and I am also a member of the Tumut Fire Control Centre performing communications duties.

On Wednesday 20th November 2019 I spent one week on a strike team fighting fires in the Grafton area, then Brian and I spent a week in Lismore fighting fires in that area.

On the 24th December 2019 we received a phone call from the Tumut Fire Control Centre asking if we could help out Braidwood over the Christmas week with night shift and give those crews a break. We ended up taking Tumut Riverina Highlands Cat 7 truck and young Liam from the Tumut brigade.

Once we arrived in Braidwood we tried to get some sleep before heading out on night shift. Most of the nights out we were the only truck patrolling and putting out fires, as everyone else was on stand down. We returned home late on Friday 27th December 2019, unpacked, washed our RFS gear and went to bed.

Saturday 28 December 2019 woke to lots of smoke in the air. By midday we were geared up and sitting in the Batlow RFS shed awaiting instructions. A few Batlow brigade members were sent out to do patrols, whilst we remained in the shed on standby. We were stood down around 7pm. Once home I received a phone call from the Tumut Fire Control Centre asking if, in the morning, I could come into the Tumut office for communications duty .

The Tumut Fire Control Centre (FCC) is located in the Riverina Highlands building. The FCC becomes fully operational under a section 44 as was the case with the Dunns Rd fire. The FCC has many people working in different areas 24-hours a day. Along with the communications and the radio, there is also: air operations – looking after fixed-wing and rotary wing aircraft and the Tumut airport; a section making sure everyone is fed and, if required, accommodated; people looking after safety and welfare; the supply and repairing of equipment and trucks; mapping; managing heavy plant and other resources; compiling duty rosters; weather forecasting operations; and team-managing the whole incident.

Not only are FCC members working in the FCC there could be other organisations involved like Forestry, National Parks, Police, SES, Fire and Rescue, and local council, just to name a few. Some of these people are paid staff and some are volunteers; some are away from their own families. Everyone in that office was working just as hard and long hours as those people on the fire ground.

Sunday 29 December I started early in the Tumut office. There was a fire on Ellerslie Road on the other side of Adelong. There were two of us on comms duty.

We were on that radio nonstop. And what most people don't realise is that I don't use a scribe. For record keeping, while I'm talking on the radio, I am writing down the conversation – even though it is recorded. Around 9 pm we handed over to the next comms duty personnel. I did manage to get home that night.

Monday 30 December 2019 was another full on day with comms. busy on the radio, with no chance to stop to eat and drink something. We were lucky to get a quick toilet break. This was the first Christmas that I actually lost weight.

My sister-in-law and brother-in-law were arriving at Adelong Carvan Park to celebrate the New Year with us. I managed to contact them and told them things were not looking good and advised them to pack up and return home to Merbien, near Mildura, which they did. It ended up being a wise move, as the fire at Ellerslie was getting bigger and there were lots of spot-over fires happening all over the place.

I couldn't get home that night, and all accommodation was booked out in Tumut; and people I know in Tumut had already evacuated. I thought I'd have to stay in my car for the night but Marie from the Tumut RFS office offered a bed at her place, which I was very grateful for. I ended up staying at her place quite a few times when I couldn't get back to Batlow. Even though I was very tired I didn't get any sleep and had trouble contacting Brian, as phones were not working properly and reception was very bad.

Tuesday 31 December 2019 back into the office early for comms duty. I did get to hear Brian on the Batlow truck and knew from the radio transmission that he was on the fire ground at Kunama and was okay. He also knew that I was okay by talking to me on the radio.

It was an exceptionally busy day for me as I was the only one on comms duty. Help didn't arrive until late afternoon when two RFS girls from Wagga Wagga arrived. This happened a few times, being on the radio on my own without any help, but I just got on with it. At the end of shift I was not allowed to go home in my private vehicle but managed to get a driver to take me home in an RFS vehicle. When I got home I did some washing and packed a bag with a few things. The following day, as my car was in Tumut, I got a lift down there with the Batlow VRA.

Happy New Year 2020

By this time Batlow was virtually a ghost town, most businesses were closed and nearly everyone had already evacuated. The smoke in the air was very thick and there were embers falling to the ground.

Thursday 2 January was my day off; Brian was out on Batlow 7 fire truck. I was at home by myself so I made sure everything was away from around the house and got rid of leaves and cleaned up as much as possible. I got a box ready with water, baked beans, first-aid kit, towel, torch, battery and my RFS gear and put them under the house just in case I had to take shelter.

Friday 3 January I managed to get down to Tumut for another shift of comms duty. Things were not looking good. Brian was back out on a fire truck around the Batlow and Kunama area. I couldn't get home again that night and stayed with Marie again. It was very smoky and hot in Tumut, and quite eerie. I kept praying that everyone and everything will be okay.

But the situation was getting worse and worse by the minute. RFS group leaders and captains were after more back-up and support, especially aircraft. Unfortunately because there was so much smoke around aircraft were grounded at Wagga Wagga airport. There was no visibility so it was just too dangerous to send them up in the air.

Heavy plant and water carts were also working flat chat on the fire ground. Again there was only so much heavy plant available, along with operators, so they couldn't always be sent to certain areas straight away. As you can imagine you just can't pick up a dozer/grader and move it someone else within minutes. You need an operator and a float to load it onto and then someone to drive that float to a new area. All this takes time.

'Fire Comm – Fire Comm – Batlow Captain – Over'
'Batlow Captain – this is Fire Comm – Send – Over'

There are those words again. The ones you don't want to hear.

Saturday 4 January – this is the day of the fire storm. The day that Batlow was deemed undefendable

But the wonderful people of Batlow who stayed behind, along with outside help, did defend Batlow. And what a marvelous job they did.

I was on comms duty with Robbo. As he is not a very quick writer, he was on the radio and I was his scribe. Communications on the radio was nonstop.

Not only was Batlow under threat but the fire was burning out of control in Tumbarumba and Adelong areas. Group leaders, captains and ground crews were asking for air support, water carts and heavy plant equipment. As the fire was so widespread it was impossible to have these resources in every area ready to go.

It was very worrying, stressful and hard, listening on the radio to where the fire was impacting and for the requests of where we needed to send more support and help. Quite often I would have rude, angry and upset people on the radio – which I could fully understand. But I could not let it get to me. I just had to keep calm and polite and tried to calm them down too.

People need to be aware that it's not up to the radio operator to make decisions and move people and equipment around. We receive the message and pass it onto the appropriate section to act on.

At one stage I heard that the fire was coming in on top of Mayday Road and for an instant I thought 'oh no, that's not far from my place'. And that was really all the time I got to think about my own house, because we were so busy; heads down, bum up and into it.

That evening, at Marie's place, it suddenly hit me what happened that day. We all had been to hell and back. I couldn't really comprehend what had happened until much later when I headed back into Batlow and saw it for myself. Being ex-army and having served over in East Timor I have witnessed horrible things and so much destruction; but it is still very confronting to see it again, especially in your own town. But I once again realised that, 'yes, while it is sad to lose your home, your possessions and your precious things, things can be replaced'. At the end of the day they are only things, we only get to have them in our life for a short time anyway, but life and your loved ones are what is important, they cannot be replaced. As time goes on, we create new memories; and the old ones are with us always.

But once again that night, 4 January, I couldn't get home. There was no phone service or electricity in Batlow, and I couldn't contact Brian. I knew he was out on the truck fighting fires and that he was okay. But I found out later that the service station in Batlow was lost, as was Wakehurst House along with houses and sheds, in Batlow and Tumbarumba. Thankfully no lives were lost.

Sunday 5 and Monday 6 were pretty much the same; very busy on the radio. After having stayed at Marie's place for a few nights I was finally allowed to go home on the evening of the 6 January, but had to be escorted by an RFS vehicle.

Michael from Batlow Brigade met me at the Batlow turn off and escorted me home. It was so strange driving up the hill towards our town. From the Adelong turn off at Wondalga into Batlow everything was black and burnt or still burning.

Thick smoke was still in the air and it was horrible seeing the lost homes and the devastation along the road towards Batlow.

Even now when I head back up the hill from Tumut to Batlow, I feel sick in the stomach and my heart starts to race; I don't know if that will ever go away.

Our house was okay. But the front garden was burnt as was the 250 m hedge. I wasn't overly upset about the hedge as it was getting very hard for me to maintain, but the garden was a shame. We had lots of rare and beautiful trees, bushes and bulbs, that are now lost for ever.

There still was no power or phones in Batlow. I didn't realise we had a generator at home so Brian had managed to keep the fridges going. He had to change over the lead from one fridge to the other every few hours. We bought a bigger generator to keep both fridges going at once and I was also very grateful that it ran the washing machine.

On Tuesday 7 and Wednesday 8 I was back down to Tumut on comms duty. I had the Thursday and Friday off, but instead of sitting around at home I went out with

Brian on a fire truck, patrolling around the local area and putting out spot fires behind AMCOR. We patrolled along Old Tumbarumba Road and put out a fire in some young burning pine near where the sugar pine was lost.

Power was restored to most of Batlow on Saturday 11 January. Those energy fellows did a fantastic job; they deserve a huge thank you. Brian and I had the day off and headed over to Darlington Point for our nephew's 18th birthday. We were supposed to stay the night for the big party but could only stay for lunch as we were both on duty the next day.

On Sunday 12 January Brian was back at the Batlow RFS shed and then out on a truck, I was now on night shift with comms, a little less hectic than day shift. My replacement in the morning didn't show, so I made a phone call to Sue to see if she could come in and do the day shift and I would do her night shift.

I was on night shift until 17 January, had a night off then did my last night shift on Sunday 19 January.

My final day of comms duty for the Dunns Road fire was Friday 31 January 2020. But, as the saying goes, 'it ain't over until the fat lady sings'.

Friday 7 February we had a fire call around 8.45 pm: Bartlett Street, Batlow, at the rear of a yard at the base of Batlow hill.

Some underground roots and hot spots had started to flare up due to the wind picking up. Then we had two fire calls on the Sunday 9 February: the first one was at 9.20 am at Springfield orchard where a little tractor/digger machine was on fire; then another fire call back at Bartlett Street.

Often, afterwards, if I was down the street in Batlow, so many people came up to me and gave me a hug and big thank you for doing such a great job on the radio. It was amazing. They couldn't believe the hours I'd spent on the radio and how calm my voice was all the time. They said by listening to me it made them feel better and calmer and they knew what was going on.

I hadn't realised they could download an app and listen in on the local RFS radio network.

It's now over a year since the Dunn's Road fire, and Batlow is slowly rebuilding, not just in houses and infrastructure but the people too. Some will never fully get over what happened; they can only learn to live with the trauma. There is help out there so I truly hope these people are seeking and receiving that help.

Straight after the fire there were many negative and horrible comments going around about how the fire was handled, that their property wasn't defended and that the RFS didn't do enough. This was quite upsetting to hear. We have heard it so many times that this fire was unprecedented and that, no matter how many people or resources were thrown at that fire, it could not have been stopped.

The RFS, 'mosquito brigade', locals with slip-ons and garden hoses did what they could do with what they had, they worked their bloody arses off and put their own lives at risk; and some of these people also lost properties, sheds and belongings.

To those negative people I say put the uniform on, dedicate your time to volunteering and see if you can do it better.

The RFS is still keeping me busy. Brian and I have helped train more than 100 students in various brigades on their bushfire course, with communications and pumping. I have been to Dubbo for a week to learn the new computer-aided dispatch system (CAD). This is a new system where RFS jobs are created and managed on a computer system.

I also spent one week up north at Port Macquarie assisting with the floods. This was certainly different from working with fires, and another learning curve. Currently I am assisting with training RFS cadets; 10 students from Batlow Technology School have joined the cadet program I am really enjoying my time on this program as I am learning a lot and gaining more experience and confidence. Plus it's encouraging to be working with some great young people and hopefully have some positive input in their lives.

Sulari on Diana Droscher

Diana and Brian came to Batlow as the new owners of the service station, and in doing so integrated themselves immediately into the day-to-day life of the town. They would run out and fill up your car long after such service had been become a thing of the past elsewhere.

Both Diana and Brian are members of the RFS, and are active in the Batlow sub-branch of the RSL. And in almost everything else to do with town they are eager participants, enthusiastically dressing up, making food, stacking chairs.

Di is possibly the most organised person in not just Batlow but the entire Snowy Valleys Shire. When the front hit Batlow, I and my fellow refugees, were in Tumut listening to the fire-coms for any clue of what was going on.

I remember the panic and horror, brigades begging for air support, new fires spotting everywhere, crews unaccounted for, and Di's voice, calm and consistent in the eye of the storm.

Not the Sunrise (Part II)   Michael Blenkins

Batlow's new Cat 1 truck was initially viewed with some scepticism when she arrived.

'It won't fit up orchard rows like the Cat 3 can!'

True, but the Cat 1 is very well positioned above the ground, can carry more water and has a deck from which a fire can be observed and fought. Steep yellow steps lead to the back seats of the cabin. My RFS overalls were a tad tight around the waist. The overalls had not shrunk over the Christmas period. Climbing those yellow steps provided the exercise I really needed.

For the first two or three days after the Dunns Road fire had escaped the confines of its original fireground, we were assigned to control burns in the pine plantation near Kunama. Areas accessed from Posthumers Road and within the pine forest were to be burned with the aid of the trusty drip torch in an effort to reduce fuel loads and provide a buffer to neighbouring farmlands.

Occasionally, the fire would race up the strips of dry bark snagged on tree

branches and trunks. Roger wisely told Edmund and me to not waste water as we contained burn offs, and to 'feather up' the burnt remnants with the spray nozzles.

When we were completing one of those control burns at Kunama, Edmund and I noticed a frightened bush rat which had sensed the fire encroaching on its territory. Panicked, the poor creature scampered out of the patch being burned to where the truck was parked with the pump motor revving. But its escape was short-lived. Setting eyes upon us, it turned in terror and darted back into the fire and hot coals, and immediately became a living torch as it died before our eyes.

This was the first of many deaths we would see, but that little rat haunted me. In the weeks that followed, the media reported on the suffering endured by animals and birds, both native and introduced, which fell victim to the fires.

We would periodically emerge from the labyrinth of barely distinguishable logging roads to Posthumers Road to catch up on any news from the main fire front. The road was patrolled by Joe and Debbie Burgess' son-in-law, Steve Horsley, who possessed a wealth of local knowledge relating to both forestry management and firefighting, would chat with news he had heard. Andrew Wainwright also called in a few times.

By this time, roads into the Batlow area had been closed and barricades were now marshalled like we were suddenly living in enemy-occupied territory. So it was really surprising that we ran into a couple of vehicles towing trailers with apiarists aboard who had driven two or so hours to retrieve their precious bees and hives before they were engulfed by the fast-approaching flame. I also well remember at a crew change when we caught up with Joe Burgess — who was not his normal good-humoured self. He had been frustrated by a bureaucracy of rules and regulations in an effort to have his cattle relocated by a livestock carrier. His phone was out of charge or range, so we loaned him a mobile phone to make a few more calls. Joe proved persuasive.

At the crew changeovers our brigade captain, Darryl, appeared calm, but something about his generous smile hinted at the weight on his broad shoulders. Jason Roberts, his faithful lieutenant for the duration of the fires, was by his side. We all joked that our RFS overalls were now fitting our middle-aged figures much better, as we'd lost weight with the heat and the days of physical work and stress.

The regular re-filling of trucks meant that large water tankers were strategically located in forests and road junctions. I recall one solo tanker driver, who I think was from Wagga Wagga, positioned in the forest somewhere near Settlement Track and Browns Forest Road — but my memory might be wrong. On the surface, the driver appeared jovial, but we could see he was nervous, which was fully understandable, as he was stationed in an unfamiliar area surrounded by huge pine forests and on-going controlled burns. His only company was the UHF radio which was forever conveying the increasingly-panicked or despondent reports and fire com communications. He quipped it would take little enticement for him leave his station in the forest to head home to Wagga Wagga. We refilled at that tanker a few times, he was always glad see the faces of RFS crews, for a chat and a momentary morale boost and distraction from what was coming in over the UHF.

Another control burn continued on roads that hugged the Adelong Creek near Frogs Hollow Road, which branched off the Green Hills and Batlow Roads. We were in a festive mood: it was New Year's Day, so we wished each other Happy New Year. Most of us were bleary-eyed — not a consequence of late-night revelling, but days of long shifts on the fireground.

These control burns were now undertaken with RFS crews that had travelled from afar to help us in our hour of need. We worked with RFS from various areas, including the Ariah Park district.

The mood along Frogs Hollow Road was tense; waiting for Forestry officials to sanction controlled back burns. There appeared to be delays — or 'buck passing' or pending shift changeovers — but as volunteers, not on the payroll, we were acutely aware time was not on our side.

A plan of attack was determined — the chatting was over. Drip torches were lit and drizzled a line of fire along the road's edge. The fire moved swiftly, very swiftly, in fact too swifty, and soon needed containment.

The blokes from broad acre flat country, who were well-versed in fast-moving stubble fires, were overwhelmed by the conditions and vast fuel loads that surrounded us. Indeed, it was a daunting task.

The sheer heat radiated from the fires gave us all a fright! Collars were turned up, gloves, face masks and goggles essential. Hoses were run out in record time and the clatter of the diesel pumps echoed in our ears as we somehow managed to control burns and tried to reduce the ridiculous fuel loads. The whole process was not without mishaps. The sides of our truck's cabin were left a little worse for wear, melted side mirror casing and blistered reflector decals. A heat-affected passenger's side door was rendered a bit reluctant to close without a generous slam. These blemishes have since become a reminder of the Black Summer fire season. The pristine Cat 1 truck was now well and truly part of the Batlow Brigade and was loved as much as the Cat 9, Cat 3s and the temperamental Studebakers from the time that were part of RFS folklore in tales recounted by the likes of Bob Bowman.

As the heat and the day intensified, and word was received of more outbreaks of the fire, we called out onto the Green Hills Access and Wondalga Roads. The fire was moving at a rate and mature pine and native trees were crowning. Updates were constantly provided about the movements of the various fire fronts.

I remember watching a lone semi-tanker drive along the road to refill at the Forestry Nursery Depot. Within a minute or so, my heart sank as we watched a vicious fire storm jump the road and engulf the trees that lined the road.

No one said a thing, our silence was horrified; all of us certain that the tanker driver and his companion were now stranded. Or even worse.

The shift finished. I drove back to Tumut to what we now called the 'refugee

house' — lent to us by Manning and now shared with the Batlow Kynastons and Wondalga Jones. The air-conditioning had stopped working and so the families had purchased half a dozen fans which moved around the hot air.

Edmund and I washed our RFS clothes and shirts; the water was quickly black with the soot. Pegged on the clothesline, our uniforms were dry within ten or so minutes, ready for our next shift.

2nd January

At the end of our day shift, we drove out of Batlow to West Batlow and entered Old Tumbarumba Road to check on our house. The pumps had ceased to run days before; there was no fuel to replenish their tanks with. The generator was also silent. Our house felt alone and haunted. We backed Edmund's truck into the driveway, so that we could make a quick getaway. The house felt strange; left in a mess of last-minute packing in the days before. It was upsetting to be in the house and knowing that it would likely be reduced to ashes and mangled, burnt iron. I remember looking at our dining room suite and my bookcases filled with books. A set of CMH Clark's *A Short History of Australia* given to me on my 21st birthday by my parents. Even more special as I had met with Manning Clark and talked with him in the rain around the campus of ANU.

On Edmund's insistence, we ventured to the garage to see if we could start my old 1969 Mercedes Benz. It had not been run for ages, but strangely it seemed to fire up okay, but idled roughly and coughed and spluttered. I quickly backed it out of the garage and as we passed my mother's old Vauxhall Victor (nicknamed Susie by my late Grandfather), I felt a real sense of guilt that I had purchased the incorrect fuel pump (a stupid Ebay effort on my part); so that Susie sat helpless, alone and stationary in the garage.

The old Mercedes, obviously also guilt ridden, then decided to go out in sympathy, and promptly stalled. And as you would expect, there was insufficient charge in the battery to kick the motor over again; so the Merc just sat there on the driveway in front of the garage. I thought of Basil Fawlty at that moment — and how he gave his stalled Austin a good thrashing with a limb in a Fawlty Tower's episode. There was no time to laugh.

Edmund arrived with our International 434 tractor and we towed the Bedford truck, which had also decided it would not start away from the house. We positioned the Bedford in front of our house yard on Old Tumbarumba Road. Once again, the face of the Bedford appeared somewhat unimpressed by the whole situation.

Acutely aware that our ten-minute mission was nearly over, Edmund and I went to his Ute to leave. He urged me to try to start the Merc just one last time. I did so reluctantly but in the five minutes since the last effort, the battery had recomposed itself enough to actually kick the engine over. With possibly only three cylinders firing, I revved the old girl harder than it had ever been revved in the decades I had owned her, and we were off in reverse. Lights on, the fourth cylinder finally firing, we moved in low and second gears, heading up the Old Tumbarumba Road at 30-40 miles per hour to the relative safety of Batlow.

Edmund followed behind, listening in on the UHF as reports on the radio mentioned a rather surreal sight of some old Mercedes making its way past the roadblocks at White Gate and at the town's edge and into town. In the back of my mind, I hoped that there was enough fuel in the car's tank, as it had not been driven for perhaps two years. I parked her in the lane near the RFS shed and Batlow Technology School teachers' carpark where I used to park her when I taught at the school in the late 1990s.

Edmund and I then headed down to Tumut. I was convinced the Police would charge me for driving an unregistered and uninsured vehicle, but by this time we were essentially living in a state of lawlessness; so the crime of driving an old car seemed petty, and I guess justifiable, given our circumstances.

3rd January

On the 2nd and 3rd January we relieved the night crews and undertook control burns. The fire was making its way out of the Green Hills plantations and into the properties that border the tinder-dry plantations. I remember being called to the Peel property on Old Tumbarumba Road, just a few kilometres down the road from our own place. We were stationed at the main house and made quick checks of gas cylinders and potential water supplies.

The bushfire was now moving swiftly up the hillside from the Adelong Creek and through paddocks. We considered cutting a few access points in the boundary fence to better defend the house from its southern side. In the meantime, flames had encircled the vast trees near the neighbouring property which belonged to the Robertson family. The house and its yard structures appeared lost.

Visibility was poor because of the dense black smoke, but the bright red and orange flames were winning the day. Roger, Edmund and I readied ourselves as we anticipated that a flurry of spot fires would hit the Peels' house and sheds from the south or from the paddocks to the west.

A new chapter of panic reigned as we realised that dozens of spot fires were igniting on the eastern side of the house — the side facing the Old Tumbarumba Road and access lane. Pumps were started, hose lines quickly run out, and the spot fires in the dry yellow grass and along the fence line were extinguished. To be honest, the rest of that day now remains a mystery to me.

The township of Batlow had been deemed 'undefendable' in the days before. The fire was clawing its way through the forests and now the farmlands to the west of the town where we had been fighting the fires. There was some talk of fire breaks being put in across the hill behind the back of Batlow; and there was even speculation of a control burn on the hill to provide a buffer between a potential (or inevitable) fire front and the town.

The prevailing weather conditions were hopeless by this time; and speculation about such a fire-management action seemed to cultivate fear rather than support and enthusiasm.

As I drove to Tumut that night, I drove past The Rock, a local Batlow property. Its fences were in fantastic order, its front paddocks were absolutely clean, there was not a blade of grass visible: cattle and sheep had been strategically relocated to those paddocks that bordered the main road. The management practices were first class.

And that made me feel pretty inadequate about our own livestock management practices — our two much-loved horses, Matilda and Kamoo — had been secured in one of our fenced trufferie paddocks. Our layman's logic was that that the densely planted Oak and Hazelnut trees would provide some protection. I thought grassy paddocks, edged by gum trees, would enable fast fire movement and cause the horses to panic and come to grief on the barb wire fences on our boundaries.

4th January

Our day shift on 4th January started as shifts had in over the preceding week: equipment was checked, supplies obtained from the huge supply of food packs and drinks that had now amassed at the RFS shed — much donated by charities in the region and kind residents who had been evacuated from the town — and the Cat 1 tanker re-filled.

Roger, Edmund and I went back out to West Batlow where we had been the day before. The morning was still and the air smoke-filled; another hot day, accompanied by strong winds by mid-morning, was on the cards. Attempts had been made to contain the fire during the night.

We entered the fireground through the Steenholdt property and ran into Frank as we negotiated the track. He was visibly tired and had not slept for days. From the boundary of the Steenholdt property, we then accessed the property of other neighbours, Matt and Rachel Galvin, and the adjoining property owned by Rodney Jorgensen. The ground was steep where the properties backed down onto the Adelong Creek and its various tributaries.

It seemed to me the mood was more positive on this day. Some D8 dozers and their drivers had worked throughout the night to put in new fire breaks. We heard on the fireground grapevine that the Robertson's house had not burned to the ground the day before. This news seemed unbelievable, as the place seemed doomed the afternoon before.

As it turned out, the positive mood was short-lived. An urgent message came through that multiple spot fires were appearing on the Old Tumbarumba Road. We were off. We made our way up to the Amadio family's property, Montello and adjoining property, Fairview. Just as we had seen the days before, spot fire seemed to start without warning and swiftly burnt large areas of yellow, crisp-dry grass.

As we arrived at the reported fire, Roger looked around and spotted the entrance gates. He re-familiarised himself with the sprays fitted on the front bullbar.

'You're on the back, Ed. Use the canon spray.'

Over the radio came commentary from another RFS member watching from the adjoining paddock: 'You won't put that out with the truck sprays!'

Roger did not bat an eye lid or even offer a witty reply under his breath. Time for humour was over and the real fight was on.

Edmund was on the back and we were off, Roger used the bullbar sprays as he drove in circles around the paddock which was now really ablaze as the fire spread. Miraculously, the Cat 1 seemed to develop the turning circle of a Mini and Roger manouvered the huge vehicle as if it were an agile stockman's horse. Within a frantic half an hour or so, the grass fire was extinguished, at least temporarily.

Edmund, wild-eyed after having been thrown around on the deck like a rag doll, re-entered the truck's cabin. As we left the burnt paddock and accessed the road, Roger grabbed the UHF hand piece and responded to the nay-sayers:

'You won't put that out with the truck sprays!'

In the meantime, the fire communications had become more and more frantic, as multiple reports came in of spotting near the Batlow Cemetery and on other fringes of the town. A firm directive was received that the Old Tumbarumba Road was to be evacuated at that point as the fire had reached the town. In all the years I had lived on the Old Tumbarumba Road, we had always thought that the vegetation and bark along the roadside would function like a 'wick' if a bushfire actually hit the road. It looked like that theory was going to be put to the test.

We hit the Old Tumbarumba Road and raced as fast as we could into Batlow. I remember fumbling with my mobile phone to take a final photo of our house as it stood surrounded by a haze of grey smoke and guarded by the old red Bedford stranded out the front on the verge.

Other RFS crews followed us in via White Gate while others headed to their own districts via the Wondalga intersection where fires were breaking out in an afternoon of sheer chaos. One of the large semi water tankers — which came equipped with two witty clowns who were always in good spirits and who had until this point worn thongs — sprinted for the town.

As we left West Batlow, I remember turning to Edmund in the cabin and telling him to remember this moment. I expected that our house would be gone in another twenty minutes — at 2.20 pm on 4th January 2021. I was resigned to this fact, and hoped, in the back of my mind, that my insurance policies were as good as they were stacked up to be.

In town we were stationed at the northern side on Wakehurst Avenue — our initial job was to monitor and protect the powerlines and transformers in case the fire hit the town.

By 2.40 pm the bushfires were howling like jet planes, attacking the town on two fronts: from the west (over the hill) and from the north (Tumut Road). The Cat's lights were engaged and flashing, the visibility was incredibly poor as the sun was obstructed by the dense black and greeny-grey smoke. We stood in Wakefield Avenue, listening to radio reports of the fire's movements around Batlow, but also between Batlow and Adelong. I recall mention of Sharps Creek and Yaven Creek. We were watching closely for any ember attacks. The atmosphere was surreal.

'Time for a group hug and prayer, fellas' insisted Roger.

I did not recall this in the Basic Firefighting Course, but to be honest it was perhaps the wisest thing to do. The task ahead was a huge challenge — and no standard operation procedure had been written for this scenario.

At 2.40 pm the town resembled a ghost town in a Hollywood Western. No people. I remember seeing a goat running around and a house with its windows covered in corrugated iron; a few sprinklers spun around, but their enthusiasm and energy seemed challenged by a lack of water pressure. It reminded me of the sprinklers and sprays I had on my own house's roof the week before.

To be honest, much of my memory from this point of the day is sketchy to say the least. We went from fires in paddocks along Cemetery Road and up into Mayday Road, to fires on buildings at the Atkinson property along Geddes Road. We worked with teams from the Wilkinson property. Refilling and fighting again.

Edmund at the front of the truck would aim the hose and direct water to douse flaming cow pats which would only reignite within seconds. We developed a system: Edmund would extinguish the main fires and I would use one of the hoses from the rear of the truck to spray the cow pats and any other fuel if it re-ignited. Hours passed at Wilkinson then Watkins paddocks, and Ray and Tina Billings. Roger knew the paddocks and a crossing that enabled us to come out onto Keenan's Road.

At one point, I remember us refilling the Cat 1 from a water tanker near Goulds' Nursery. Despite the chaos, our mates with the tanker semi-trailer were still in good spirits and cracking jokes, but they had now abandoned their thongs for work boots and other PPE. Metres away the spot fires had entered the grounds of the old cannery and thick black smoke billowed from excavators and other equipment which had caught fire. The noise of the howling wind and fire was by

this time accompanied by the sound of exploding gas cylinders! I had initially assumed it was the LPG cylinders on homes on the western fringes of the town, but the explosions were actually coming from cylinders at the rear of the service station. Crews from the town brigade were attending to the fires at the service station and the house on the adjoining block was well alight.

We re-filled at a standpipe near the junction of Heatleys Road and Forsters Road. I was controlling the valves on the truck and in the confusion, turned the valve to shut rather than open. The pressure caused a hose to explode in rather a spectacular fashion.

The tall trees along either side of Gedyes Road

which branched across the narrow road, were alight. The darkness of the bleak and eventful afternoon now continued into the night. But the absence of sunlight meant that the spot fires were easier to see.

We fought through the night: sheds at Harvey property, check on Baron property, gates were locked at the McCorkingdales' Cascades Nursery. Paddocks near Forsters Road with Billy Watkins. Then Forest Road where fires had started behind the houses, and the vegetation along the creeks and gullies and into Mill Road was alight. Fires along Keenans Road — the pines that line the rear fence of Bob and Jenny Bowman's property were on fire and created a frightening definition of the road.

We started to drive up the steep driveway to the Kynastons' property, Fairview. But from our vantage point just off Keenans Road, the situation appeared hopeless: huge flames raged behind the house and lack of a turning circle, meant that the check had to be reassessed. Roger pulled up the truck near the gate after gauging that the house was lost. The fire raged behind the house nestled on the hill, which itself appeared to be on fire. The distinct smell of an old fibro garage at Newnham's property on Keenans Road. We ended up at the Garner property.

The slip-on brigades were busy as the fire attacked the fringes of the town and then followed creeks and vegetation which followed gullies and creeks through the town.

We were exhausted. Edmund had a blood nose at some point, and Roger was knackered. The decision was made to call it a night and reassess the damage in the morning. Back to the Batlow Fire Shed. We had assumed that our place had been lost and so we planned to stay at Roger's place for the night or the hour or two before dawn, anyway. I went out to my old Mercedes turned on the diesel motor to let the engine warm up. The RFS shed had had a close call in the course of the day. In the meantime, another call had come in and Roger and Edmund headed out for one more firefighting stint at the end of Pioneer Street in a house that had been a shop.

I sat in the car listening to the ABC new broadcast, received updates on fires across the nation and tried to text my wife in Tumut. Next thing I knew Edmund and Roger were at the car, saying that we were calling it a night and going to Roger's place to get a few hours' sleep. I thought they had been gone for ten minutes, but they had been gone for close to an hour

We slept on the floor — a rolled up RFS jacket is a perfect pillow.

Stoney Ridge 4ᵗʰ January

Douglas Rand

The fires came a year ago today
And in an hour they torched our mountain down to rock and earth and silence,
And blackened trees lying where they fell, like soldiers on a smoking battle ground
Or bowing, still in stunned submission to the rush of wind and flame...

And through that aftermath we thread a path
Once familiar and well clothed in grass and eucalyptus,
Wildflowers and bird song,
But now its modesty all burned away – laid bare.
We wonder, will anything remain,
And would we yet see fruit of prayer,
Or the labour that had raised our house
And raised our kids.
What kind of shattering still lies in wait around this corner,
Hidden in this acrid shroud?

The fires came a year ago today
And took us down to rock,
And in a year ignited wonderment;
So, stone on stone, and brick on brick,
We rise again,
The same,
But different.

Sulari on Douglas Rand

I was first introduced to Douglas as a colleague of my husband. He was the French teacher at Batlow Technology School back then, and like us, a blow-in who'd chosen to make a home in Batlow.

He and his wife Belinde, a nurse, built their beautiful mudbrick home overlooking the Goobragandra Valley, where they raised two daughters and a son, as well as goats.

Doug is perhaps the most positive person I've ever known. I have not once heard him say a bad word about anyone, even those who deserve at least a few bad words. He is truly a gentleman.

Like Tourists in Our Own Town　　Amber Jones

The songs and the poems consider fire analogous to love. 'This love is like wildfire,' they say. 'We're afire with love,' they sing. They are wrong. I never want to hear a refrain like 'you set my heart on fire' ever again.

Three families, two dogs, one house. Have we been here for three days or three months? Time is no longer real. It passes fast and slow at the same time. The air conditioner doesn't work. We spend days trying to figure it out. Flushed faces and limbs glisten with a constant sheen of sweat. We drape the dogs in wet towels and pat them in front of the fan to keep them cool.

Smoke looms ominously, weaving itself into the fabric of our clothes and dulling our vision. It creeps into lungs already choking on panic. Niggling coughs, scratchy throats. Sharp inhales of the Ventolin grandpa insisted I take home with me at Christmas. I took it to be polite, thinking it would forever stay unused at the back of the medicine cabinet. He was wiser than I gave him credit for.

I wear the same three shirts on perpetual rotation. Every sweltering day feels the same, each one blurring together into one never-ending nightmare. We spend every waking hour compulsively refreshing Fires Near Me and checking the news. The sky glows orange all the time now. Maybe Y2K believers were a couple of decades off. It certainly feels like Armageddon.

We spend afternoons at the laundromat, like tourists in our own town. Sitting on the cold tiled floor listening to the industrial machines spin our clothes clean. I wish I could climb inside the soapy barrel too. Maybe if I'm spun around long enough, the anxiety will wash from my chest. It already burns like bleach up my trachea, so I'm halfway there.

I can't stomach the thought of food. Too hot, too anxious. It's too hard to cook in a house that isn't our own, so we eat at the pub. We listen to the heroes, fathers, husbands, sons in our midst tell us what they have seen up on the burning hill. I've never consumed more beer in my life than that summer.

On the worst night, we cram, clammy, into the room downstairs. We listen to the RFS scanner and the wind howling at the window. There are loved ones on the frontline that nobody has heard from in days. The nerves are nauseating. Gradually, we hear the news. Three houses and the lifetimes of memories embedded in their walls, gone. Anguished tears and heartbroken hugs. My childhood best friends facetime me. None of them are here, and I'm not sure if that makes it better or worse. 'At least everyone is safe'. We hang up the call and I cry.

Overnight, a miracle is granted. Somehow, despite the odds, all three houses were spared. Breakfast that morning flips from sombre to joyous the moment that everyone shares their good fortune. My family's home is the closest, and in the least affected area. We choke down McMuffins and terrible coffee and tell half-truths about feeding stock to sneak back into the evacuation zone. We assess the minimal damage and marvel at our luck.

Ironically, the kitchen is flooded from the sprinklers leaking through the ceiling. There are a couple of burnt fenceposts and the lawn is littered with blackened gum leaves, but everything is otherwise untouched. There are empty water bottles shoved into the tennis court fence where RFS members had stood and watched the flames roar down over the hill. Even as I stand in their dusty boot prints, I cannot fathom being in their shoes that night.

Armed with hoses and shovels, we all band together to put out lingering smoulders near the creek and on our neighbours' property. It's hot, the smoke is suffocating, we're covered in flies. Everyone ends up with wet socks, filthy clothes, and ash-smeared faces, but it's the best I've felt since this all started.

Maybe fire is associated with love, but not in the way that you think. It is not romantic. Fire causes suffering, grief, hurt, and trauma. But sharing those lived experiences so intimately with others fosters connection. Intense bonding. Love.

Sarah on Amber Jones
Amber has been a life-long friend of my eldest daughter. I've had the privilege of watching her grow-up into a mature, intelligent young lady. She has the rare ability of really listening to and engaging with others of all ages.

Our families have shared many afternoons at the Batlow Pool, BBQs and cuppas at each other's houses and of course kids' birthday parties.

Our lives, however, became more intensely entwined during the fire than any of us could ever have imagined as Amber so eloquently describes.

Wet Stuff on Hot Stuff

Edmund Blenkins

So, my story starts in the heat, a day as relentlessly hot as every day of those eventful weeks. I am an apprentice electrician at the local mill — bottom of the food chain. I was working our yearly Christmas shift, replacing and fixing the broken and forgotten parts of the mill ready for another year of production. I was wiping my brow after completing a job in the reclaimed shed, when my little blue chirping box started sounding its song.

I looked down: 'Firecall — Batlow RFS region'.

I quickly started my clumsy panic of packing up my tools, then dropping them, and then packing them up again, before realising my first mistake — not asking my tradesman if I could respond to the call of the blue chirpy box. Because, as I've been told before, 'You do not breathe without consent as an apprentice!'

He responded to my question with a classic Aussie: 'Bloody oath mate, you go! I'll see you tomorrow'. Wish I could say I saw him the next day but sadly it was the start to the longest and shortest two weeks of my life.

My first day crew: Roger, often called 'my dad' by the rest of the crew because of similar cheeky attitudes, a man I'd go on to fight the rest of the fire with; Starch, the old wise bloke who would often joke about keeping Roger and I separated as we were 'bad news together'; and Captain Coop, a name given to him due to a simple mistake made on paper.

I did as most teenage boys these days do: I Snapchatted my entire approach to the battle ground, safely aboard the untouched, unscarred, brand new Cat 1 tanker. God, I love this truck.

Approaching Laurel Hill, something hit me hard. A cereal bar. Rog had thrown it at me.

'Get off your phone, boy!'

I sat the phone down and started to observe the field, putting my training and experience to use. Yep, I had no fricken clue what I was looking at, but look I did.

Thirty minutes pass. You don't really see a fire coming in the pine forest. You see smoke, then you see a dusty green smoke, and then the trees start to look sick, almost as if they know their doom is on the doorstep.

We pulled back to the homes off Cobden's house, about a kilometre off the Green Hills access road. We approached gate after gate (two) and because I was the youngest, I had to get out and open them. I didn't forget to remind the rest of the crew that I don't mind helping senior citizens. We pulled into the back paddock of the house yard and watched as the fire grew closer. Then we jumped to action, I grabbed a hose off the reel and started putting out spot fires. Took me a solid 10 seconds to realise I couldn't see the truck anymore.

'Get back in the truck, boy!' Roger called out.

'Where is the bloody truck?' I yelled back.

After a bit of coughing and tearing, as my body was not yet accustomed to the taste of an Australian battlefield, I found the truck and climbed onto the back with the cannon. Roger then chased the fire, using the jets on the front of the truck to cut the flame and I followed through, killing it with the jet much like a gun and bayonet: the gun used to give the initial blow and the bayonet to finish the enemy off. The fire got ahead of us; smoke surrounded us. I climbed in the cabin as we headed to our new location, still high on adrenaline. We were bouncing up and down in our seats like kids catching the bus to school. Then–

'Jesus Christ' screamed Starch.

Directly in front of us in the smoke-filled paddock stood a grader – I kid you not – no more than 10 cm off the bull bar of the Cat I. The smoke was so thick we didn't realise that we weren't even in Batlow anymore, let alone in front of a bloody grader.

There we lined up across the road, like soldiers in a trench.

We prepared our cannons facing them towards the ever-approaching fire but the flames swallow an entire field in seconds. I remember the raw heat pushing towards my face, the wind carrying the almighty fire towards us, the flames bearing down like a charging bull.

Pumps on, cannons open, the pressure throwing my feet into a steady stance. The first jet stream of water turns to vapour before it even comes into contact with its foe, like they were dancing around each other before a fight to the death. Seconds go by, the trenched trucks positioned on the battle line of no-man's land are firing away.

'Boy! Stop wasting water!'

I was confused. Wet stuff on hot stuff — this is how I assumed a fire was fought, this is how I've always fought fires. I cut the cannon off and turned towards Roger who was pointing across the road.

'Jesus Christ, how in hell did it get over there?'

Somehow, in the few seconds I was fighting the fire, it jumped over me and was attacking the other side of the road. Surely my perfect battle plan hadn't failed?

Wet stuff on hot stuff.

I came to the conclusion that it must have just been another fire. No way it could have got past me! Wet stuff on hot stuff never fails.

After several attempts, we managed to direct the beast away from the homes we are trying to save, but it still wasn't stopping. We pulled back to the Green Hills Access Road turn-off and were met by some ambos. I was coughing smoke, my lungs still a virgin to the new environment we were in. I was sent from the truck to go grab some fresh masks, met with kind faces offering all the assistance they could. Before I could even thank them I had ice cold water poured all over my face, six masks in hand and I was turned back towards my truck.

We headed to David Hawkins' home on Green Hills Access Road, sirens wailing as the 13-tonne battle truck pushed through the front line. We pulled into Mr Hawkins' driveway, sat the truck next to his house, and jumped out to spot the approaching fire. Wind was hurling its might across the field.

'Cut the bloody fence!' Roger called out.

The fire was moving so fast you could compare it to the speed of a race car. I ran into Mr Hawkins' shed and grabbed a pair of bolt cutters and headed outside.

'Not the fucken Fergie,' cried Roger as he ran for the pump.

I grabbed a hose — second nature now — and ran towards the old tractor, and doused its surroundings with a layer of water and foam.

'Stop wasting water Boy!'

Again I was confused. Wet stuff on hot stuff.

I retrieved the bolt cutters as I brought the hose to the back of the truck and started winding it up. Thank God I was on the one truck in the fleet with an automatic cable-reeler.

Roger grabbed the bolt cutters off me and headed for the fence. Sorry Mr Hawkins, I thought as Roger cut his fence line. And then, as if it had just spawned there, a grader came out of nowhere and cut a deep line around Mr Hawkins' house.

We headed back to the Greenhills Access Road turn-off and waited for the change-over shift. Once they, we all piled into the ute. All except Roger, who made it clear he was staying to continue the fight and jumped back in the truck.

As we were about to leave, we ran into Darryl, our captain, and, more importantly, Roger's big brother. Starch explained to Darryl what Roger was doing. Well, Darryl stormed after the truck, and Roger, with a wrath similar to the fire. I wasn't there for the conversation, but I'm pretty sure it went like most conversations between younger brothers and their older siblings because Roger came back to town with us.

Day 2, 6 am we head out to Tumbarumba Rd where we exchange with what was last night's crew. Their exhausted faces explain more than words. Today, the fire chased us, hounding us from the forestry camp. It was vicious and ruthless. Without any notice the whole pine plantation was on fire. The green that we are all used to, now black and red as the fire and engulfed once proud trees.

Because my memory seems to be all over the place from these few days, the next thing I remember is that we were lined up from the road down into the forestry entry beside 7 Springs. A back-burn had been ordered, so some of the boys started getting the drip torches going. A little army of men started lighting up the bush, including my Uncle Phil. He's not technically my uncle, but we've been family since I was a baby. Within five minutes it became apparent that we had used a little too much fuel. We'd created a monster — a fire to fight all fires!

Well, it got kinda hot and the little lane glowed red from the flames. If you ask me, Uncle Phil melted the truck; ask Roger, he'll tell you the same story: Uncle Phil melted the truck. We sat on the fire for the rest of the day

Another day same fire, 8 am. We boarded the Cat 1 again out in the bush, meeting up with the night crew, who looked exhausted. I was riding with Roger and my dad, who is best defined by the fact that he wears business shirts under his uniform and carries a pen into battle.

So, today's adventure: we start on the other side of Batlow. We roll through the bush patrolling the edges of the fire. Little did I know this was going to be the quiet before the storm. We drove up and down forestry roads, enjoying the fresh fruit that had been supplied to us by the people feeding the firefighters. I guess living off lollies and chips for four days makes you appreciate the finer things in life.

Roger was still on me: 'Boy, stop wasting water!' He was even onto Dad about it. We were controlling a back-burn that was controlling the fire.

That night after we had changed shifts, Dad and I went out to our house, a few kilometres out of town on the Old Tumbarumba Road, to try and collect some of our household goods. By the time my mother had evacuated, there'd been no time to do much more than run, so we'd left everything behind. We swung back through town afterwards to see the blokes at the shed. Dad spoke of his poor old Mercedes parked in our garage and how sad it would be to lose her.

Roger said, 'Go get it then.'

Dad, being the law-abiding citizen he is, replied: 'But it doesn't have any rego.'

The laughs of the crew filled the shed. We were in an abandoned town which had been decreed undefendable, a place where fire trucks ruled, and Dad was worried about the expired rego on his classic car.

So Dad and I headed back to the house. I hooked my winch to the old girl and started pulling her out of the garage. Once we had her out Dad dropped some fuel into her tank and started kicking her over. The engine made that dead whining noise, but Dad was determined. 'Bang!' the old thing went and Dad, foot to the floor, revved the guts out of her in an attempt to keep her alive. Yep, about two cylinders were firing and that was it. The holes in the exhaust amplified the fact. But Dad was off, heading to Batlow at 20 km an hour, though I wasn't sure if it was because of the car or because that's just the speed that Dad drives at. By the time we got to town it sounded like he was at least running on three cylinders in the old rig. He pulled into the fire shed and you could hear the laughter of the blokes over the sound of the exhaust.

B-day. Batlow Day as I like to describe it. I can only assume that the actual D-day was as crazy as our B-day. Ours started on my home road of Old Tumbarumba Rd. Dad and I had come to accept the idea that we would lose our home. We were sad

but there was nothing we could do. Even though we had a petrol J2 Bedford ready, with two pods, and a slightly flogged-out pump, we weren't quite sure it would be enough to fight this fire. In any case we didn't have any breaks in which to save our place, because it was all just go.

Roger drove the Cat 1 down the back of Steenholt's/Browns' place— the property next to ours — where we were met by a huge dozer clearing a break. We sat and observed the beast of a machine as we waited for the approaching fire.

Then it came. A sound like a jet — deafening, crackling, whistling and roaring.

We were called out of the bush and back to the road. The fire had jumped just down at Peels Creek. We drove to the turn-off for Honeysuckle Lane.

Three trucks just sat there, watching the fire encase the fire.

A bloke yelled from the window of another Cat 1: 'You can't fight the bloody thing!'

Roger replied with a classic smart-arse response 'Watch me'.

Roger told me to jump on the back of the truck again; my new home now, as I wouldn't be leaving my nest for the next 10 hours.

Cannon in hand, Roger turned on the quick sprays on the front of the truck. We circled the fire and brought it down, slamming it with hundreds of litres of the wet stuff.

'Oh Jesus Christ!' I yelled as I was thrown metres in the air!

'Sorry, Boy, found a wombat hole.'

'She's right, Mate.' I realigned my helmet.

We continued to push the fire down, Roger driving straight into the flames with cannons blazing, as we doused it. Roger drove back to the road smirking: 'You can't fight that bloody thing'.

Then the radio called to us: 'The fire has jumped and is heading to Batlow, Exit Old Tumbarumba Rd and return to Batlow'.

This was a dark moment for my father and me. After feeling relieved that we had succeeded in stopping one spot fire, it now all seemed useless. It had managed to get around us and we were now abandoning our own home entirely, to protect the town. Oh well.

We lined our battle trucks up at the entrance into town and waited for the crackles and whistles to get closer. We made a few phone calls as the radios were telling us that all crews were stuck in Batlow, and we had no air support. We weren't sure if this was going to be our last day.

Dad, Roger and I stood in a circle and had a huddle.

'Righto boys, we got this,' Roger said.

I guess Dad and I looked pretty hopeless at this point, so Roger decided to lighten the mood, grasping poor old Dad's backside. Dad yelped and we all cracked up, in good spirits again. The fire grew closer, and we loaded up onto the trucks and started to disperse around town.

Before we knew it, houses were on fire everywhere. We were racing backwards and forwards dumping water on anything we saw that was hot. I restrained the use of the water as I had finally learnt to not waste it.

I was sparingly soaking down a grass fire when Roger gave me a look of joy: 'Wet stuff on the hot stuff, Boy. Let her have it!'

Well, I reckon I had a smile from ear to ear. I pumped the pressure up and let the son of bitch have it! Load after load, we filled up at the Cowboys' semi-truck, and we let the fire have it!

'Slow down, Roger!' Darryl called on the radio as we were taking the great beast of a truck around winding corners. As most brothers do, Roger waited until we were out of sight of the Fire Shed before speeding up again.

'Boom!' The ground shook. An absolutely massive explosion. We drove towards the clouds of flames in town and, on approach, realised that Batlow no longer had a servo. We filled up with water again and headed back out the road. I watched from the back of the truck as the old cannery came crashing down in flames.

Dad jumped on the back of the truck with me. We started pushing the fire back on a paddock. Back and forward up and down, for hours. We didn't stop once. Then it happened.

Nothing I have ever seen could equal it. The winds swirled the fire into a burning tornado. We chased it around and around, smashing it with all we had, taking its fuel and, eventually, bringing it to a stop.

We stopped to refuel the water tank at a standpipe. I started connecting the hose up but before I could finish, Dad turned her on. Well, I've never seen a hose fly so high. After having a quick chuckle and connecting a new hose, we ventured back into town and started chasing house fires.

There was no further talk of not wasting water. We knew it was now or never.

Sulari on Edmund Blenkins

This is my son, Edmund. He was born in Tumut Hospital and raised in Batlow. Edmund joined the RFS when he was 16, and at 18 was one of the youngest to see active duty during the Black Summer fires.

Having volunteered to join the fight in Northern NSW in November, he'd only been back a couple of weeks when the fires were on our own doorstep. Edmund will tell you he's a sparky (electrician).

He went into Black Summer with all the invulnerability of youth, thinking he was 'ten-foot tall and bullet proof'. He came out with evidence.

The Devil Dog

Jessie Caton

The Devil Dog licks its ember-dripping tongue among the screaming trees.

Blinding all with its burnt paws and choking fur.

The sky above and the sight below, sulphuric as if under cannon fire
in some great war.

Buildings crash and melt under the blasting lungs of the red-black beast.

Humans lie dead curled up where they fall.

Red Devil dogs have loped across the continent since the dawn of time.

There was no easy death as the fiery dog waxes and wanes.

No ease as its jaws snap and its claws slash.

Our land is burning, searing, hot, dancing with agony.

Our land is dying, twisted black pines dead and sunken with grief.

But... there are those who stand.

They are Valiant.

They are Dejected.

Terribly steadfast,

Horribly exhausted.

But standing there,

Not a flicker of doubt or denial.

Standing soldiers with reflective
orange and yellow armour.

And when the great smoky beast
begins to wilt, they are the ones
who become truly strong.

Our Land has burnt

We call.

Our land is dead.

We sob.

The Devil Dog growls its last
fiery gust.

There feels no ease in living.

Though we gather together,

Stranger and friend.

How do you rebuild a life that spanned an eternity?

How can a heart begin to love again?

When before us lay the skeletal remains of a community that lifted its head,

Proud that impending doom, that was,

Ever to be our never!

Can we gloss over that pain?

The unfairness of that deadly dog?

Yes we found a way.

Love, goodness and hope.

New Friendships.

Hope and memories.

Before the choking fiery hell wrought itself upon us all.

Memories of gentle greenness.

And trees reaching high a splendour forever to our minds.

Sulari on Jessie Caton

Jessie lived at Laurel Hill near Tumbarumba for over 20 years.

The Sugar Pine Walk , the iconic stand of trees planted in the 1920s which grew to form a kind of living cathedral, and to which all locals proudly dragged visitors, was just a brisk step away.

Jessie's A Frame house did not survive the fires.

She and her mother evacuated to Wagga where they stayed for nearly a month, before renting a house in Tumbarumba.

Two years on, they have bought a wonderful place on the Murray River, 30 minutes from Tumbarumba.

The Best and the Worst

Rob Ironside

I remember thinking in the leading up to New Year's Eve 2019, that it sounded like the fires that summer were going to be pretty bad, so I decided I'd put our water tank and pump, or the slip-on unit as they're referred to, on our old Hilux ute, just in case I might need it at short notice. A day or two later, on 30 December at the Batlow RSL, there was a community meeting held by the local fire authorities. At that meeting, we were all told that it would be best not to be in Batlow tomorrow, on New Year's Eve, or New Year's Day, because of the apparent fire danger.

At the end of that meeting, as we were leaving, a friend said to me, 'So, are you staying?'

I said, 'Yes.'

He said, 'Why would you?'

I said, 'To look after our home and keep an eye on the neighbours' places'.

I thought if the fires did come through as they'd predicted, our local firies could probably use all the help they could get.

On New Year's Eve after my wife Cara tried hard to convince me to evacuate to Gundagai with her, the kids, my father and another local family, I decided I was staying. My eldest son, Jordan, also decided to stay in Batlow.

I admit I was feeling very uneasy about the whole thing as we said our goodbyes and they drove off to Gundagai.

I went into the backyard and started hosing around our shed and shortly after I spotted Dad coming into the backyard, which was a surprise as I thought he was leaving with Cara and the kids and the others. I instantly assumed he was coming to try and get me to go with him.

So, I said to him, 'If you're here to try and convince me to come with you, you can forget it.' And he said, 'No, I'm staying here as well.' And that made me feel a lot better.

The fires didn't really impact Batlow on New Year's Eve, and the family and our friends returned on New Year's Day. At which point they decided they wouldn't evacuate again if they were advised to, and we'd all just thoroughly prepare and plan for what sounded like was going to be the worst of it in three to four days' time.

The police and the fire authorities and local government officials held another community meeting on 1 January at the Batlow RSL Club. That meeting changed everything as far as I was concerned. There was an extraordinary number of police there, which kind of made me think, this isn't just going to be an information session or an update session. There was more to it than that. So I decided to record the whole meeting.

It was at that meeting, for the first time, that I heard Batlow described as being undefendable.

I don't think any other town in New South Wales or Victoria during that fire season had been referred to as undefendable. I can understand why the authorities took the tone that they did at that meeting. They were basically saying there was

going to be major damage and loss of property and potential loss of life. I guess they wanted as many people out of Batlow as possible, because they didn't want hundreds of unprepared panicked people trying to escape or evacuate at the last minute, or when the fires were at their worst.

I still think the message could have been delivered differently. I felt awful for all the very upset residents at the end of that meeting. I was just plain astounded and angry that our town was considered undefendable. I felt like they'd given up on us.

I sure as hell wasn't giving up on our town, and I'd hoped that there'd be other people feeling the same as me.

At the end of that meeting, as people were leaving, I noticed a lot of women crying, they were that upset and scared and frightened. I was just plain angry. As we were walking out, the same friend that previously asked me if I was going to stay said: 'Surely you're not staying this time?'

I said, 'Yes.' He said, 'You're mad.'

Obviously, I didn't quite agree with that. But I could tell that my wife, Cara, seemed a bit rattled and, when we got home, I knew she was worried about what had been said at the meeting. When I asked if she was now having a change of heart about staying, she said she was.

I told her it was probably better if she went then, because if she wasn't confident to stay, I didn't really want her or the kids around. She said that I should also evacuate with them now as well but I said I wouldn't be leaving. That resulted in a fairly lengthy and emotional discussion.

At one point there, she said to me, 'You think you're bigger than the fires. You're not. These fires are bigger than you'.

I realised I had to bring the conversation to an end, so I said: 'If I evacuate and one ember blows up under the ridge capping of the roof of our house and smoulders away there, and nobody notices it, and the firefighters are too busy elsewhere... Well if something like that happened and our house burnt to the ground, I would never forgive myself for leaving, and I would never forgive the person that made me leave.' She then accepted that I was staying, no matter what.

Over the next couple of days, we packed about a week to 10 days' worth of provisions into two four-wheel-drive utes and prepared the slip-on firefighting unit on the ute. We put that many provisions together just in case, like if we had to camp out at the showground or something.

I went round and blocked all the house and shed downpipes and filled the gutters with water. My son, Jordan, made similar preparations around his house, and my father said he was going to stay with us and help defend. My dad was nearly

81-years-old then, and I reckon that was a brave decision on his part, to stay in Batlow throughout that whole Dunns Road Fire event.

I set up soaker hoses all along the rails of our front and back verandahs, and watered all the gardens around the house, and filled the bathtub with water, and prepared our little generator. Basically, we prepared everything that we thought we might need in those days leading up to when the fire was due to hit us. At that stage, it was supposedly 4 January.

On 3 January, Cara and the kids headed down to Tumut to stay in a friend's house, who was away at the time. I remember my youngest son, Carter, desperately wanted to stay with us in Batlow and help. It was bloody hard telling him he couldn't stay, but I really wanted him to be with his mum and sister in Tumut, to hopefully help keep them calm, and look after our dog that was going down there with them.

On Friday 3 January, after Cara and the kids left, we spent most of the morning checking we had everything packed, and that we had what we needed. Jordan and I went down to the local supermarket to grab a few last minute bits and pieces, and there were PRIME7 TV news reporters out the front of IGA, speaking to locals as they were coming and going from the shop.

They asked if we were staying to help defend and I told them we were, so she asked could she ask us a couple of questions for that night's news program.

Her first question was, 'What do you think about Batlow being described as undefendable?'

I said, 'I think that's nonsense, and if you went down to our local firies' shed and asked some of them that, you'd find there'd be a lot of those blokes who would strongly disagree; and may even be highly offended by that statement'.

Her second question was, 'Do you think the township of Batlow will still be standing tomorrow?'

I replied, 'Are you serious? The whole town can't instantaneously combust all at once. And I'm sure the firefighters here will be able to save most of the town, no matter how bad it gets.'

I really wasn't impressed with her negative line of questioning. Needless to say, those questions and my answers didn't end up making it to air.

One really important thing over the couple of days leading up to January 4 was the scanner-app that allowed us to hear all the local firefighters' radio comms. We were constantly listening and it was a great comfort to be able to hear what was happening and where it was happening in the lead up to those fires.

On the morning of January 4, we were fairly relaxed considering what was being reported throughout the media. Everything was prepared and planned, and it was pretty much a waiting game now.

A friend of ours, Luke Hilton, who lives only a couple of blocks from us, had also stayed, along with one of his neighbours, and they were calling in periodically to check how we were going. I told them we were pretty right, and that if it got to the point where we could see flames topping trees in the bush behind us, over Tumbarumba Road, we'd evacuate down to the bowling club and tennis court carpark and wait there till the main danger period had passed. I told them they were welcome to join us down there if they wanted. They agreed that that was probably a pretty good spot to hold up if required.

By midday, we were completely prepared to defend and/or relocate downtown if need be. I was getting up onto our roof every half hour or so to try and see which direction the fire was coming from. By about 1.30 pm, I could see huge plumes of smoke rising from the northern and southern outskirts of town, and there were several waterbombing helicopters and aircraft flying around above town.

At 4 pm, Dad decided he would leave his place at Bartlett Street and come and join Jordan and I down at my house. By then, we could see dark smoke rising from different spots around town, and I believed, sadly, that this smoke was probably coming from residences and buildings on the edge of town that had caught fire.

Some time around 5 pm, I heard one of our local firefighters on the scanner say something like: 'It's just jumped the Batlow Road, we've lost it.'

That was tough; I kind of just felt gutted. Not so much from what he said, but from the tone of his voice. I felt terrible for him and all those other firies that were trying to contain and battle that monstrous blaze. I mean, what an enormously difficult and dangerous task for all of them.

Not long after that, we could hear the roar of fire to the west of our place. At that point I decided I would start videorecording the events that were about to unfold. I put my phone in my shirt pocket, with the camera lens sitting out above the top. Moments later we noticed flames topping the trees directly behind both Jordan's and our house, so we decided it was time to turn the soaker hoses on around the house and evacuate to the tennis court and bowling club carpark.

We got down there without incident and Luke Hilton and his neighbour turned up soon after. We put our facemasks on as we were concerned about what might be in the air. By this stage, the smoke all over town was so thick and dark that you could look directly at the sun, which just looked like a dark red dot in the sky.

I remember a lady with a few dogs in her little car came driving into the carpark as well. She looked pretty stressed and asked, 'Where do we take all the animals?'

I told her I didn't have a clue but that she could stay with us and she'd be all right. I also suggested she leave her car running with the air conditioning on recirculating air, and wind the windows up, and that I'd come and hose her car down from the tank on our ute if it got really hot and if it was required to help keep her cool.

I realised then there were quite a few vehicles in that carpark, so I suggested we should reposition some of them to allow fire trucks access through that carpark. So we did that. Another car with two fairly distressed-looking people drove in. I went to see if they were okay; they were journalists for the *Daily Telegraph*. I told them that we had plenty of cold drinks and water and stuff there if they wanted or needed, and they could wait it out there with us. I told them the same thing about leaving the windows up and the air conditioning on, hosing their car down if things got pretty hot.

They obviously felt a little bit more comfortable after a while, and both got out and took some photos of the five of us and asked us some details about who we were and why we stayed in town. That discussion ended up becoming an article in *The Daily Telegraph* later the next day, I think.

By around 6.30 pm, the wind was blowing really strongly across the carpark. It actually got so uncomfortably hot we started spraying water on the legs of our jeans and trousers, just to keep ourselves cool.

We assumed it was the nearby old Mountain Maid Cannery, which was well ablaze at this time, that was creating the heat where we were. Over the next half-hour or so, we could also hear huge bangs, like explosions, which turned out to be gas bottles exploding at the local service station. That was very unsettling as we were anticipating that these exploding gas bottles would be causing huge amounts of damage. (We later found out that they didn't.) But I can remember dearly hoping, when we could hear those explosions, that the huge gas tank onsite at the old Mountain Maid Cannery had been drained or emptied.

At 7 pm we thought the main fire front had passed by, so decided we should go back up to our homes and assess any damage; and assist in putting out any spot fires that we came across on the way.

Luke and his neighbour went to their places to check them out. Dad waited at the tennis court and bowling club carpark with the lady and her the dogs. She was concerned her house might be gone, so she asked if we would check her home on the way up or on the way back for her. Which we did, and it was okay.

Jordan and I went to check ours and our neighbours' houses. Ours were okay, but we noticed the house three doors up had fires burning in the backyard. So we went up with the ute with the slip-on unit, and I think spent 15 minutes putting the fire out in that backyard.

While we were doing that, Robert McVean came down to the back fence to assist us in whatever way he could. He lived across the road. He was so cool and casual about the whole thing. He was standing there, happy to chat to us about the local cricket competition and people's scores and batting averages and that sort of stuff. It was really quite odd. We thought it was amazing how calm he was. Looking back, I think it was good, because his demeanour probably helped calm us down a bit.

While we were there, we noticed a small fire next door in John Quarmby's backyard, so we put that one out. Then, just as we were leaving there, we noticed another fire had started in my next-door neighbour's front garden, so we went down and put that one out too. Then we headed up to Bartlett Street to check Dad's place. His front strainer post was ablaze like a giant candle, so we fairly quickly put that out. We noticed another fire smouldering in the backyard of the place next door to Dad's place, so we put some water on that one.

By 8.30 pm we were back down at the bowling club and tennis court carpark to pick up Dad and let the lady with the dogs know that she still had a house to return to. We headed back up to our house.

When we got there, Jordan noticed smoke rising from a neighbour's backyard on Sunnyside Avenue. We drove the slip-on unit down to the bottom of our place and jumped the fence into their backyard, and we put that fire out. Or so we thought.

After that, we went home to discover that there was no power, and very little phone reception, so we started up the generator, mainly just to keep the fridges cold and heated some dinner on the barbeque.

At 11 pm Cara messaged me asking us to check John Melrose's place on Sunnyside Avenue. So we walked down, and it was okay. But, as we were returning, Jordan noticed the fire in the backyard of the neighbour's place, that we thought we'd put out earlier, had flared up again. We went in, grabbed their hose but there was barely a trickle. After checking the hose and its fittings were okay, it suddenly dawned on me that the town had probably run completely out of water. We managed to get that fire out with the trickling hose, then went home and decided to get into bed. It was about 1 am.

Dad said he wanted to sleep on a mattress outside, on the front veranda, rather than on a bed inside the house, which surprised me. I asked him why, and he said, 'It would be cooler out there, and all the smoke would keep the mosquitoes away as well.' I wasn't so sure about that theory. Anyway, the next morning, he said he'd slept fine, so I guess he was right.

The next morning, I was getting text message after text message from Cara, forwarding requests from concerned locals who had evacuated and were unable to get back into town. Understandably, they were worried about their homes and property. They were asking us to go and check their houses, feed their cats, and chooks, and horses, and water their vegetable gardens etc.

We spent the next two days, flat out, doing that, checking people's homes and animals and gardens and businesses. In retrospect, I think it was good we were being asked to do all that stuff, because it took our minds off what had just happened, and kept us occupied, both mentally and physically. And it was good to know that we were providing some peace of mind to all those people.

On Tuesday, three days after the fire, we went out to check our grazing property on the outskirts of town, only to find every inch of that property had been burnt, and all the fences had been destroyed. We were luckier than others, we didn't have any property or sheds, or any livestock of our own out there at that point. The open pasture areas were completely black, and littered with burnt carcasses of kangaroos and joeys.

It was an awful apocalyptic scene.

On the way back into town, as we were coming past Cemetery Road, we noticed a ute, with an assortment of items on the back of it, pull out and quickly race up behind us. As we were passing the old swimming pool site, we were passed by three police vehicles in a row, heading in the opposite direction, out of town. I noticed all three did quick U-turns and pulled over the ute travelling behind us.

I thought it was a bit odd, but we heard later that the people in that ute had been looting some unattended homes around town. Talk about the police being in the right place at the right time.

I guess we got to see some of the absolute best and worst in people in those few days of and after the fire.

In the days between January 4 and when the townsfolk were allowed back home on January 8, Batlow, for the most part, felt like a ghost town. I'd be happy never to see or feel it like that ever again.

I would have stayed to defend our town and home regardless, but to have my

father, Jim, and son, Jordan, there alongside me throughout that dreadful period, is something I'll always appreciate greatly.

And I can't adequately describe the feeling of overwhelming happiness that came over me when my family and most of the other residents of Batlow were allowed to return on January 8.

I'd never experienced anything like the Dunns Road fires in my lifetime. One of the most important things I learned from that experience is, when it comes to responding to the threat of bushfires, having a well thought out plan, being thoroughly prepared, and being able to hold your nerve, are of the utmost importance.

In the months after the fires, on a few occasions, I've been asked by people if staying here in Batlow during the Dunns Road Fires had affected me adversely.

They said things like, 'You stayed, during the fires, didn't you? Are you okay?' Or asked, 'How's your mental health and wellbeing?' Or, 'Do you think you might be suffering from anxiety or depression?' Things like that.

I've answered those questions as honestly as I can. My responses have been along the lines of: 'No, I think I'm okay', and 'I genuinely believe that my mental health and wellbeing would have suffered more, and that I probably would be suffering from anxiety or depression if I had not stayed here with my son and father during those January bushfires and the days thereafter'.

I'm honestly glad we were here to experience it, and glad that we were able to help.

Sarah on Rob Ironside

Rob's great-grandparents, Samuel and Amy Ironside, moved to Batlow in 1922, to work on the Tumut to Batlow railway line, and thence the Batlow to Kunama line.

Rob and his wife, Cara, settled in Batlow 21 years ago and have happily raised four children here, meaning five generations of Ironsides have lived in Batlow for 100 years.

Rob is a calm, measured and practical man; someone you're glad to have at your back. He brings those qualities to bear in many situations, not least the fire.

Actively involved in the community in many guises, Rob has been president of the P&C, a stalwart of both junior and adult cricket clubs and, since the fire, the group 'Do It For Batlow'.

Robert's father, Jim has recently moved back to Batlow, and has taken up residence in the family home, that was built over 90 years ago and stayed to help during the fire at nearly 81 years of age.

A Dragon's Tale

Kathryn Masterson

The speed of light from the past
Wills us to walk amongst trees again
To breathe again, to try again
Sweet sorrow and a sunset to remember

Keeping Busy

Kylie Boxsell

I realised that this was really serious on the Thursday before the 4th. It sank in for me, then. I was pretty calm — I think I had it together and was simply so busy organising everything and just rolling with it all.

The message from RFS was to get out, that we were in great danger. I guess I struggled to believe that. I knew that we had some good resources in town, and so did the blokes on farms. I did have faith in their skills. But by Thursday, I just went, oh, shit, this is really serious.

I left Batlow on Friday morning. I was still trying to get people on buses out of town and having blues with some of the oldies because they were digging their heels in – adamant they were going to stay in town. I found I was having really, quite serious arguments.

I offered to take them out of town myself if they didn't want to hop on the buses. I tried anything I could to get them to go. It did get heated a couple of times. I guess a lot of people who were staying really didn't realise how serious it was. Some of the older residents were saying things like 'I'll just die. I'm happy to go'.
I said, 'Well, you're putting somebody else's life in danger. When somebody comes to try and save you and help you, that puts them in a dangerous situation.'

Eventually they'd say, 'Okay, righto'.

Both my girls have a very strong connection to Batlow, and Jasmine's actually moved home; well, she's moved down to Tumut now. But yeah, she's wanted to come home for quite some time. During the fires was a very difficult time for them because they'd left on the 28th to drive up to the Gold Coast. They'd just got there and, because of the news, wanted to come straight back. I don't know what they were going to do, but they wanted to be here.

I was saying 'Don't come home'. But they were worried about me because I was still in town on the Friday morning. They're saying, 'Gosh, Mum!' because they're listening to everything that's on television, and it's only showing the very worst parts.

So with everything that was going on, that I was trying to deal with, I had my girls ringing me constantly as well. It was really hard for them to be away. But certainly, and in many ways, I think, if anything, they've got a stronger connection to Batlow.

When I evacuated, I went to Wagga, because I felt I could be more helpful to the community. Obviously, everyone was being directed over there, and we had 50-odd Vanuatu boys head over there as well. I don't know the numbers, how many people we had in Wagga, but I just felt that I could tap into the resources for people if I was over there. I could have stayed with Mum and Dad in Tumut, but I truly felt that I could be more helpful in Wagga.

I hadn't packed to leave Batlow until the Friday morning, and stuff that I took was ridiculous. I grabbed a box of photo albums, and I had a backpack with just a change of clothes in it. I was just kind of walking around my house in circles.

Robyn, the president of the board, was going to stay in Batlow, and I said, 'No, no, you're coming with me, jump in the car and we'll head out.'

When we got over to Wagga, we stayed with a friend of mine. That evening for dinner, we cooked a lovely steak and some salad and I asked our host, 'Have you got any salt and pepper.' He said, 'No, I don't'.

And then Robyn pulls out of her bag, the gigantic wooden salt and pepper shakers she'd taken from her house— because that's what she grabbed. She's like, 'I've got salt and pepper!'

We went to the Equex Centre and from there, everyone was just directed to some accommodation. When I went there for the first time, it was not what I expected. I was imagining stretchers out on the netball courts. [Laughs] The same sort of thing I was seeing in the club [the RSL] with animals and bedding and swags. That's what I was expecting when I got over there. I didn't realise – I mean, I wouldn't know, I've never been in that situation — but we were being directed to four-star accommodation in Wagga and being put up in a motel room for three nights. Then it was extended for another two nights.

I got to know the Catholic College there, Kildare. That's where all the donations were sent to, and I assisted them, dropping donations to anyone that needed supplies. Keeping busy, trying to help was my coping mechanism, I guess.

There were plenty of times when I broke down in tears where it just got a bit much. But it was important for me that I kept busy.

I came back into Batlow on... I think it was the Wednesday. I tried everything to get back into town, made all sorts of phone calls saying, let me in. And in the end I got back in when the roads were still closed.

It must have been the 9th, because I thought, I'm going to have to get into our freezers at the club, because everything might be off; I'm thinking, oh, gosh, this is going to be awful. And this is what we were doing, we were chasing each other with chickens' feet. I think we were all a little overtired and delirious by that stage. So yeah, we were doing these silly things.

But I got busy and organised a community barbecue on the Friday. I really felt we needed something to come to. And it wasn't about how much damage you had; no one had to fill in a questionnaire before walking in the door to pick up supplies. It was just an opportunity for people to come together. And it was a great way for me to really reconnect with the community.

And it was incredible. I got a phone call from the Sikh crew* in Sydney, who did amazing vegetarian meals, and they asked: 'Is there anything we can do?'

I said, well, actually, I'm organising a barbeque, so it would be fantastic if you set

up on the front lawn. You can use our facilities for whatever you need. And thank goodness they came, because we were inundated. People really needed to come together. I was so overwhelmed with the number of people that came.

The Institute, where they had all the supplies set up, organised to bring up water and all sorts of stuff for the barbeque. We even had the army boys there.

And then COVID hit in March.

We'd only just got our Sedgwick Shield Social Bowls Club happening again. It was bringing people back together. We had 100 people over at the bowling club on a Wednesday afternoon, having a beer together, just having a laugh, and just, yeah, really a debrief about everything that had happened.

Because of COVID we had to take that away from them. That was really devastating for me. The club was closed for 70 days, and that was heartbreaking.

I think people in all of our community organisations are getting frustrated that we're not moving forward as quickly as they would like. There's this opportunity to tap into all this money and to get things happening, but things are slow. I do see people getting really frustrated, and I think, yeah, there's been some relationships damaged. There's a lot of frustration at the moment. Things like as you drive into town, our little park there has lost its bridge. I mean, none of that's been replaced or cleaned up, and that's the first thing that you see. Every time I come into town I'm reminded. Stuff like that, that just hasn't been dealt with.

There're still people getting teary. I was talking to somebody last week who was having a bit of a cry. It's certainly not business as usual.

Sarah on Kylie Boxsell
Kylie is a local with a strong sense of community and a desire to give back to the town. The manager of the Batlow RSL Club, she is vivacious and funny with a strong spirit of adventure. These days this mostly takes the form of long (very long) weekend hikes but in the past saw Kylie embark on an around Australia family adventure in a van with two very young daughters.

Kylie is an old friend, so we decided to get her story in the form of an interview. What evolved was an informal chat with many tangents, much laughter but also tears as the three of us relived the fire and the tsunami of emotions that accompanied the experience.

* Volunteers from Guru Nanak's Free Kitchenette in Sydney arrived in Batlow on January 10. They supported Kylie's barbeque at the RSL, and stayed for three days providing free fresh vegetarian food for breakfast, lunch and dinner.

Sweet Caroline

Cheryl Crouch

She came to us in Autumn
In the year 2021
She was long and sleek and slender
Our relationship has begun

We watched in awe and admiration
As she sidled through the gate
Our eyes as wide as saucers
As we stood beside our mates

Great beauty stood before us
Daring us to touch, explore
Our hands and eyes were hungry
And we all cried out for more.

We walked around in wonder
As we waited for the toss
Of course we knew that first in line
Would always be the boss

We watched his smile grow wider
As his loving hands embraced
All the curves and angles
Of the familiar forgotten place

Carefully and slowly
She responded to his touch
She purred and trembled beneath him
Till it all became too much

He smiled in satisfaction
As he thanked the powers that be
For she would not be here at all
Without their generosity

No doubt that she is beautiful
Isuzu — top of the line
Our big Cat 7 is here to stay
Our own — Sweet Caroline!

Animals in Every Direction

Lorene Cross

After being told the fire was getting close — and still so hard to believe this was happening — I decided to put the word out and ask people to come and help us to evacuate our animals we have here at SMART animal Sanctuary.

I couldn't believe it when people started pouring through our gate with floats, cat and dog crates etc. What a mission. We had people and animals going in every direction. My main focus was to just get them out, no time to be sorting names etc, I figured I could find all that out later.

We had cars everywhere, flashlights running around fields trying to catch donkeys, camels, horses, cows, alpacas, etc. The camels decided they were going nowhere and just sat. There was no way they were going to move. A couple of donkeys and most of the horses were removed. Any leftover farm animals we brought into the house paddock so we could try to keep them safe.

We decided if it got out of control we would open the gate and let them all go.

The cattery and dogs were all gone which was a relief. I sent two of my dogs, that I knew would follow me everywhere, to a friends at Wagga and kept my others here locked in the house.

Once we were sorted with the animals and had removed everything around the house that could burn, we got to work on our plan A, B and C. Tony is very good with fires so I and our two adult children Floyd and Tessa were all looking to him for advice.

We had a 1000-litre water shuttle on the ute and we went out and did drills using this so we all knew what we were doing and how it all worked. We also had a spray vat full of water ready and waiting.

During the first fire Tony was home by himself as we were stuck in town. He managed to fight the fire off with the help of our neighbour, and saved our large camel shed.

The second front was scary. We stood looking over the neighbour's property waiting for it to come. There was smoke everywhere. Waiting was the worst part as we were not too sure what we'd be up against. I was speaking to our neighbour while we still had phone service and she told me the fire was on them. A little later she called and said they were ok but it was coming our way.

We cut our neighbours' fence and decided to start fighting it on his property. We managed to move his cows to safety and started our battle. All day we were running from one fire to the next. The sky was orange and the air thick with smoke. When the fire was very close we decided to open the gate so the animals could run if they needed to. It was the hardest thing I've had to do, as I said goodbye to my bunch especially my boys the camels.

After a while we were getting quite good at the fighting and were feeling confident we could beat this beast of a fire. What an awesome team we had, just the four of us, no firies, just us. We battled for about six hours and then finally got on top of things.

The camels spent their time coming out of the paddock and eating my garden. But every time we raced past in the ute they would run back into the paddock as though they were saying, 'it wasn't us'.

The next three weeks of no power or running water, and limited phone service made it a very interesting time. We were not allowed to go to Tumut to the shops so started eating everything in the pantry. Boy, we had some amazing meals lol. Finally, IGA Batlow was open and there was also a shop in Batlow set up for the people who'd stayed and fought the fire.

The four of us were on fire duty each night. One would go out and patrol for an hour then come home and get three hours sleep while the others took over. It was exhausting but hey, who could sleep anyhow. Trees were falling all the time and that noise became a familiar sound. Power lines were down and security for properties was being tried by the unruly, who had decided to take advantage of empty farms.

I was getting lots of messages from people worried about the animals they had left. So Tess and I were busy each day checking animals on peoples farms and houses. We were feeding and watering chickens, cats, dogs, birds, sheep, horses, etc. It was nice to ease the minds of the people and send them pics to show their loved furbabies were ok.

Finally the townspeople started coming back and the clean-up began. We were lucky as we only lost some grass and a little bush. Others not so.

It's something I never want to go through again but would do it at the drop of a hat, especially with my awesome family by my side.

Sulari on Lorene Cross

Lorene and her family founded the Snowy Mountains Animal Rescue Team, which has, over the years, saved thousands of lives. They have rehomed dogs, cats, horses, donkeys, and camels and rehabilitated native wildlife.

In doing so they have also found best friends for countless humans.

Lorene herself is a force — a blend of practical skills and true connection with the animals who share our homes and our country.

The Community Spirit that Saved a Town   Dr Joe McGirr

As the Dunns Road bushfire burned across the electorate, we saw scenes of devastation and despair, but we also saw bravery, determination and strength.

I have been privileged and honoured to inform the Legislative Assembly about the impact of the bushfires in parliament and have also been proud to also share stories of the recovery and renewal of the Snowy Valleys, particularly Batlow.

Even now, I remain in awe of the heroic efforts of those who chose to fight the fires, not just the members of the Rural Fire Service, but also those citizens who, faced with the unimaginable, made the decision to stay and defend their properties.

The citizens of Batlow and beyond are still showing incredible strength and resilience as they work through the recovery and renewal process.

Since the bushfires, I have kept my parliamentary colleagues appraised of the initial devastation and the ongoing recovery. Some of what I reported to parliament is extracted here.

Speech to the New South Wales Parliament on 26 January 2020

'I want to recap some of the statistics of the bushfires that affected my electorate. Today marks the 29th day of active firefighting across the Wagga Wagga electorate. As of Monday, the Dunns Road fire, which began following a lightning strike on 28 December, burned through 333,940 hectares. This includes over 125,000 hectares of national park, more than 92,000 hectares of State Forest, and 113,000 hectares of private land.

'But I want to speak about the communities affected because those figures do not capture the trauma, particularly in the towns. If we look on a Rural Fire Service map of the electorate, we will see a large area of black. That is the burnt area. In the middle of that we will see a couple of white spots. They represent the towns of Talbingo and Batlow.

'As the blaze forged a path around Batlow on 4 January, I believe there was a deep scepticism that the town would survive. I was very grateful to receive a text of support from the Premier on that day.

'I remember a discussion that evening with the people in the operations centre, who believed that the town would not survive. But the work of the firefighters, the community members who chose to stay, and the volunteers kept the flames from passing through the town.

'Although I am advised that close to 50 homes have been lost there, the town has survived. I was able to visit Batlow the very day after, with my upper house parliamentary colleague Wes Fang. The scene was extraordinary. We drove in through a smoke-filled horizon of burnt trees and of scorched, dying and dead stock. There was no noise, there were no birds; it was just smoke and ash.

'When we arrived at the town, we saw that the service station and old hospital had been burnt. But people were there; people had stayed. They had defended the town and it was intact. People's emotions were pretty raw. The firefighters were absolutely dazed; they could hardly speak. And yet the people who lost houses, the people who survived the windows blowing in on them, the people who survived the fires coming up to their doors, who pushed the embers landing on their front verandas back into the garden to save the town, were still helping others.

'Despite the trauma there was a sense of hope. I will never forget the courage of the people I met nor my gratitude to them.

'Last week I was at the RSL Club in Batlow, having a discussion about an aspect of the recovery process, when a lady came up to me, looked at me and burst into tears. She had not lost property but she is part of a group that lives with a constant sense of overwhelming anxiety, uncertainty and hopelessness, punctuated by episodes of terror.

'Those feelings are experienced by people in my electorate and, of course, all the other electorates that suffered the fires. For many, this trauma will trigger depression, guilt, shame and grief. I do not believe there is one person in New South Wales who has not been affected, but many in my electorate have been very badly affected. We need to put health and wellbeing first in our efforts.

'From the ashes of tragedy comes camaraderie, heroism, and stories of courage and sacrifice. This was an unprecedented catastrophe that shocked the world. Some 5.4 million hectares have burnt, which is almost four times more than the previous worst season this century and the season is not finished yet.

'But it could have been much worse.

'In moments, firestorms created their own weather and engulfed entire hillsides. The land's red demon roared and terrorised even the most hardened, but our brave working heroes denied this fire monster more carnage, and I thank them.

'Firstly, I thank the volunteers who battled the blazes in this hell on earth. Many of the Rural Fire Service brigades and SES units across my electorate had been sending staff across the State months before. When they were called on to defend their own homes they were supported by firefighters from across the State. I particularly acknowledge the leaders of those brigades, Captain John Scott in Talbingo and Daryl Watkins in Batlow.

'I finally speak about healing and recovery. Communities can be repaired. They can rebuild and they can be stronger than before. It is important that this fervour that we have seen during this time is maintained throughout the tough months and years to come. As life moves on and media interest fades, our communities will still be struggling. They will be struggling economically because this has been a real deep cut. The communities I represent will feel the economic effects for decades. It will take years to rebuild tourism and agricultural industries. However, we have to think in terms of decades for the orchards of Batlow and the softwood industry.

'People will be struggling psychologically because they know the time it will take for scars to heal, but I believe hope is the key.'

Address to the Legislative Assembly on 27 February 2020

'Despite the imminent threat of the Dunn's Road fire Batlow's community spirit was strong. It was that same community spirit that saved the town on 4 January, embodied in the firefighters and local mosquito fleet (slip on brigade), who battled the blaze, as well as the business owners, who threw open their doors to shelter those who remained.'

Sulari on Joe McGirr

When Dr Joe McGirr became the State representative for Riverina, even those of us who'd voted for him had few expectations that we would see him very often. After all, Batlow was just a little hamlet over a hundred kilometres away from the powerhouse of Wagga Wagga. We had become accustomed over the years to not being front and centre.

But Dr McGirr has proved to be absolutely a local member. In the confusion and heartbreak that followed the fire front, Joe was with Batlow in every sense, listening, comforting, helping and representing.

This anthology has been restricted to the stories of those who resided within the 'Undefendable', but for Joe McGirr we have made a popular exception. I hope that speaks for itself.

A Bit of a Fright

Darryl Watkins & Jeff Kynaston

(Transcribed from Oral Account)

Darryl: On the Sunday afternoon I left Tarcutta at 6 pm and we went right around the fire, and I thought they had it under control, BUT... somebody didn't look after it during the night, and that's where it got away. And we just moved on from there. We just kept chasing it all the way back. All the way to Batlow. That's when it got into the forestry.

On the Wednesday night, New Year's Eve it did the huge run past Willigobung. Dates and times are just blurred, it was just — it seemed like one day.

We had 25 or 26 in the brigade at the time. And the slip-on brigade. We went around the slip-on brigade and made sure that everyone had shovels on their utes; that everything was strapped in properly, so nobody was going to get hurt; that the trailers were safe. Then we got ourselves ready, tried to work out teams and that sort of thing

Q: So with all the other brigades coming in, did you have advance notice and do you have jurisdiction over them or do they all operate separately?

Darryl: If the group captain's not here, Jeff or myself are in control. He was away tied up with Hume forest so it was just Jeff and me. We allocated them, wherever we wanted them to go. We knew where we could put them because a lot of them came from down around the flat country, around Temora and The Rock and Wagga. We just had to watch what sort of country we put them in. Put them on gravel roads and that sort of thing in the forestry where we knew they could handle it.

But on the 4th, it was just a free for all, some were out at West Batlow and I called them back into to town; they were everywhere. Everyone just came and did the best they could at the time.

Q: Was there a moment when you thought this is it, this is over, we can't stop this?

Darryl: Yeah, when the fire went over Tumut Rd, I said to them, that's it, we'll never hold it now, it's got too big a front on it. It had five different fronts on it when it came into town. it went back through Kunama. There just wasn't enough people to deal with it. Even though we had a lot here, from everywhere Brungle, Goobagandra...

Q: Did you think, when it did that run past Willigobung and towards Tumbarumba, that it was gone and we were OK, or did you all know it was going to come back to bite us?

Darryl: I thought we were pretty safe, we had done a lot of work. We'd back burnt in behind Dodd's and all over, but the trouble was we'd back burnt underneath and once it got into the crowns, it went everywhere.

They called me back to town, I don't know what night it was, Monday night I think, I was in the big truck with three other blokes from Batlow. They said 'Get into your ute and see how far it's gone.'

Jeff was at the Willigobung turn off. I was 20 minutes away. From when I left Pearce's to when I got to Willigobung, it had gone past there, It beat me. So as the crow flies: 10km in 20 minutes.

The only people in the shed — when it's on it's on — are the ones filling tankers and they're just as busy as the crews outside, because they've got to keep on getting water. But when the crews come back in, we talk to each other and have a drink and have something to eat. Once you get back to that shed you have a feed because you don't know when you're going to get the next feed. We were fed pretty well, but some days. I did 23 hours one day.

Q: Which has got to start affecting you physically, mentally

Darryl: Yeah, it was just lucky that was at the end, cause Jeff helped me. We just shared. I went home and had a sleep and Jeff looked after it. There comes a point when you just have to sleep, you just have to go home. But also the adrenalin kicks in and keeps you going, but then you're exhausted after that.

Q: Was that a big comedown after the fires because you lived on adrenalin for eight days straight?

Darryl: It was a bit hard to get to sleep for about a week after, probably. You're running around doing so much, running hoses and graders and all that kind of stuff and then you come down to doing nothing — just sitting in the shed talking to each other.

That was probably the best thing, wasn't it? Just talking to each other afterwards. There was a lot of people there, and we were lucky because not one of us got a scratch or a burn on us. Out of the whole lot. One or two of us got a bit of a fright now and then!

Pretty hectic for a day or two there wasn't it?

Sulari: A good title for the book: A *Bit of a Fright*.

Q: What was the worst moment?

Darryl: Ahh – probably when it came over the town hill at us cos once it went over the phone tower, it kept going down through Gilmore. That was pretty horrific. It went from Greg Mouat's probably to Purcell's straight through there, that was the main front. And that was when it took all the houses out on the Tumut Rd.

Q: So were you aware of that, on that kind of level: so-and-so's lost their house?

Darryl: No, no. We didn't even find that out until the next day or the day after. We were just trying to do whatever we could in town, to save what we could.

Jeff: When the petrol station exploded that was a pretty big wake up call, you know we thought... Yeah, I was just going around the pub corner when the big gas tank exploded. It blew the ute sideways when that went off

Q: So that was one of your 'bit of a fright' moments?

Jeff: Yeah! Bit of a fright. It was amazing that nobody was hurt.

We all go on about training, but if we weren't all trained like we've been trained, probably somebody would have got hurt. That's how professional people in the RFS are these days.

Everyone's... we're very lucky to have a brigade like we've got in Batlow. The professionalism in it is unreal.

Q: But then you were also dealing with a lot of people who were not trained.

Jeff: We were pretty lucky with all of the young fellas, they had a bit of an idea. The slip-ons were all really good, they've all come off farms anyway, so they've got that experience and they're locals as well.

We had them under radio control all the time; they all had radios. We were checking in all the time or by phone, but nobody told them where to go it was just wherever they could find a spot to put out, they put it out. You'd go down a street and if you saw someone there already, you'd go to the next street.

There were a lot of gardens alight in town, so the slip-ons were just running around putting the gardens out. We were chasing all the houses and sheds that were on fire with the bigger trucks.

It was bad at the time, but it's also done a lot of good for Batlow. A lot of people have got all cleaned up, new house and shed.

Q: If this were to happen again, are there things would you take into the next fire, that you didn't know before.

Darryl: I don't know. We were pretty prepared I thought.

Jeff: There's not much because every fire's different. They're talking about a bad season now because of all the undergrowth, we won't have the crowning, but we've got the undergrowth.

The problem we'll have this year is there's no roads open. So we've got to watch in the forestry, roads are washed out, culverts are washed out, trees are on the road. Just got to watch, make sure you've got an access out.

Q: One good thing, with all the rain, all the dams are full.

Jeff: Yeah, and everyone's woken up now, put staunch couplings on their tanks, so we can get water out of tanks at their houses and that sort of thing.

Q: So you think the community has learnt something from out of the fires?

Jeff: Yeah, they have. At the afternoon tea we had for the town, a lot of people said they were relieved they went to the last meeting before the fire. It put the fear of god into them and they were all packed up that next morning and they were all gone. Which was a good thing.

The only bad thing was they let people back in again too soon. We were still busy, but people were ringing 000 for stupid little fires. You know there was a couple of fires on the Snubba here and everything was burnt around them so they weren't going to do anything or go anywhere but people kept ringing in about them. People were scared but I reckon it should be another two or three days before they let people back in next time.

Sarah: From our perspective, not being here, and not knowing what had happened and it had seemed like forever, it was just this continuous blur of stress. We weren't sleeping or eating so wanting to get back was totally understandable. I was desperate to get back and see what was happening and I suppose it means people were there to black out around their own houses

Darryl: Yeah I suppose.

Jeff: But see the SES wanted to come up from Wagga. A bloke came and saw me, and I said yeah you could go around all the houses and just check. But they weren't allowed back in. Which would have been good. Someone with experience and training would have been good; even just checking people's pets.

We could have said you've got this section, and you've got this and it would've saved us lots. And checking for smouldering, a lot of things were still smouldering afterwards. Our place didn't stop smoking for three weeks up the back of our place

Q: So on the other side, what's the best memory, because there were good as much as bad.

Jeff: I spent a week with Andrew Hockey, each night shift and I'd never really met him before. I'd seen him at the fire shed but only twice, and we just got to know each other and put trust in each other, and we all got a lot closer to the other members of the brigade.

We go to a meeting on a Monday, and you might go to a fire once every three weeks or whatever but when you spend every night under extreme stress together, you've got to joke.

Q: After the fires there was a huge surge of feeling for the RFS and everybody wanted to join. Have you seen that translate into people actually joining?

Jeff: I think now we've got eight new ones.

The town came together at the right time for us. We've had a lot of donations out of this, and some big donations too, which will go back into the brigade, and a new truck! We were very lucky. We had a good lady on our side and she got us a new truck from Flemington Markets. Yep, can't thank Flemington enough.

Q: Was there any damage to any of the vehicles?

Jeff: The CAT 1 got a bit singed one night, melted a mirror.

Oh, and a cow knocked a door out of line on the 7, that was all. The cows were locked up in a paddock and they'd run out of water so the crew stopped to put some water in the trough. Someone – not mentioning names – belted a cow on the bum and she took off backwards and knocked the door as she was going and then it wouldn't shut properly. You've got to laugh about it.

Q: How did you guys deal with all the media attention that was on Batlow particularly the brigade, during and after the fires. Was that weird?

Darryl: While the fire was on, they shouldn't have been allowed in. They were in our road. Everywhere we went they were in the way, so that made me a bit cranky a couple of times.

Jeff: But after it was a bit of a break. The reporters would come in and everyone would chat; it just broke up the mood. And it put us on the map for a while.

Q: Did you have enough food?

Too much food, at times.

It's funny sometimes you didn't have anything, other times there was just food everywhere.

Q: Well we had two people living away say 'we don't know how to help, here's $50 in your bank account, go and buy food for the brigade'. So I'm sure that happened to other people too.

Darryl: Yeah, and there's good people in Batlow too. One night Joy and Kenny Greenwood brought us down quiches, they'd cooked at 3 o'clock in the morning. But everyone, just the whole town, just brought food after food. An Indian lady at the garage, Kenny's wife, she cooked us chicken. The pub was good, they cooked hamburgers one night. I didn't get there but others did.

Jeff: We were going to go but the fire started up again at the back of the shed, when a big pile of wood went up. That was after the main fire had gone through.

There were a few clowns sitting in the shed, and they nearly got burnt out! But they didn't have anything to put it out with because we had all of the hoses out. They had to rig up a bit of a thing so they could put the fire out.

Q: So in the actual heat of the main fire were you thinking there was going to be far more houses lost in Batlow in the end tally than there actually were?

Darryl: Yep. When it came over that town hill, I had a look around and I thought what's going to be left in Batlow?

Q: What was the final count for house loss in Batlow and immediate surrounds?

Darryl: I think it was 45 houses. Along the road to Tumut it was about 80% of them burnt. All of the old stuff along there is gone. And Wybaleena, the old stable out there it all got burnt.

Q: It all seemed very random; brick houses copped it worse than others.

Darryl: It was just a case of a house being in the wrong spot at the wrong time or an ember landing.

I asked the fire inspector about the Besser block houses and he said it needs 1600 degrees to disintegrate a Besser block.

So that fire must have had that much heat as it went through there to melt the blocks down to just pile of sand on the ground.

When I saw the fires going up over your place Jeff, I thought nope, nothing left there. And then when you said it was still standing I though Phew, Thank God for that.

Jeff: The berry patch saved us because it was really green, so slowed it down and diverted the fire.

Darryl: That's what saved me here too. We had bare paddocks and the firies could chase it down pretty quick. They were spraying down my hay shed, and I said don't worry about the shed, save your water and chase it down before it reaches my house. You can rebuild a hay shed much easier than you can rebuild a house

That was another good thing, we all lost sheds and stuff but none of the fire fighters lost houses which was good cos we were looking after everyone else's. That was one good thing when it was past, we still all had a house to live in.

Jeff: I was surprised at the low level of damage after the fire.

Sulari: So what do you attribute that to?

Jeff: The training, the professionalism and the slip-ons because they put out a lot of houses. They went everywhere, they were behind us all the way.

Q: So why aren't some of those in the RFS? Is there a reason?

Jeff: Have you met the captain?

Darryl: Yeah, that's probably why! But also we didn't have all our eggs in one basket.

Jeff: The slip-ons were able to move so quickly while the town brigades basically had to stay in one spot near the hydrants and couldn't go far. The slip-ons were going to street to street, and our units too, the sevens and the nine.

Q: How crucial was air support. Did it play a big part?

Darryl: We only got one helicopter. Tumut got the fire retardant laid down — $200,000 worth – and we got none. RFS made the decision. They'd already decided we were undefendable, so right from the start nobody would worry about us.

Jeff: But you couldn't get air support anyway, it was just too smoky.

Q: Any funny memories?

Jeff: Me asleep under the tree and the others poured a box of empty beer cans around me and took a photo.

After the fire went through all the power was out, so we couldn't have hot showers and we were so dirty.

Darryl: I was a bit worried, I had a bath after Jeff and he didn't wash the black rings off — but we were in the creek.

Jeff: That's what I was going to say about you but you were too quick!

Darryl: Some of the boys went over to the swimming pool, had a bit of a swim, took a cake of soap.

Q: So the Batlow RFS were washing in the Batlow pool! Did anyone take photos of that?

Darryl: No but I wish they had! I said, 'you stupid idiots, if you wanted to get in I have a swipe card in my ute, you could have opened the gate. You didn't have to climb over the fence! The shire might lock us all up for illegal swimming!'

Actually straight after the fires I think if you wanted to murder someone in your RFS uniform you'd would have been alright. That was the time to do it. You missed your opportunity

Darryl: I thought about murdering someone, but I won't mention any names.

Q: What surprised you the most out of everything that happened?

Jeff: The speed of the fire on the Wednesday night, and the fact that they were saying earlier that it would impact Batlow on the Saturday. But it had already gone past. They said that's when it would be worst and we were looking and thinking, what's left to burn? Because there was nothing left.

Darryl: Everyone expected to come back and not have a house. We have to thank a lot of people too, like the bulldozer and grader drivers.

Scobes needs a big thanks. He had three dozers and two graders. He started at Posthumers Lane and did right through to Gilmore Creek, and rows around houses. The Bowdens, Justin with that skidder, he was just doing tracks everywhere.

And young Ricky Ryan down the back of Old Tumbarumba Rd. Ricky was out with us and lost his own house you know. They're the people you've got to thank.

Darryl: Joe McGirr was bloody excellent through the fire. Every time he was in town, he came to us.

Jeff: Yeah actually, every politician that came, came with a camera crew. I was at the shed one day by myself and he came up, no one else and just came up and thanked me. And after the fires too he was at the institute for the start of the recovery.

We had absolute admiration for people on the other end of the coms because that would have been one hell of a job.

Darryl: Yeah, I felt sorry for them too. John Gregory especially, because he's got us all out here, and he doesn't know if we're hurt or not and he's ultimately responsible for all of us. So thanks to him because he did a good job through it all

Goobragandra and Brungle, they were here right through it all and after. A lot of good brigades who came to help.

Q: Do you think that the 'undefendable' tag made things harder for us because people had given up on Batlow?

Darryl: It made us more determined to save whatever we could. 'I just said well we'll try our best and we'll just do what we can do.' And we did.

Which was way more than anyone expected.

The Trees of Batlow

Ivy Hilton

When it rains, raindrops fall,
  Off the tree's leaves,
    Onto the ivy covered wall.
When it snows, snowflakes drift down,
  The trees are bare,
    A blanket of snow covers the ground.
When the sun shines bright,
  The trees are green, the days are long,
    But then light fades into night.
When it is windy, the wind howls loud,
  Blowing the leaves on the trees about.
When the fire is here, the trees turn black,
  The leaves are gone as the fire cracks.
The fire is over, the trees regrow,
  The bright green leaves begin to show.
    Hooray! They saved Batlow.

Between Christmas and New Year in 2019 the dry lightning came — the thing we all feared.

The east coast is on fire. Looks like it's our turn now.

The new year came and went and the pine forests are all gone, the hardwood is all burnt.

We'll not see it the same, not in our lifetimes.

Homes and farms are burnt, we all did the best we could, then fought for the town.

With one hell of a fight, some luck and good men, the day was won.

Hope we never have to face anything like that again

As the years roll along, may the story be told.

May parents tell their children what happened to us here.

How the hellfires came to knock on our doors and how all who fought became legends around January 4.

A Rainbow Gate to Batlow

Kathryn Masterson

Hope is ahead and our hearts are in the valley
A climb of faith through visions of despair
Ringing out in these mountains
Protected by the skies that bring her rain

Undefendable

Sulari Gentill

Recollections and live social media posts

We'd dropped my father and Atticus at the Wagga train station early enough in the morning for Dunns Road's beginnings to be a distinct glow in the predawn sky. Dad was going from our annual Christmas gathering to some event in Melbourne. Atticus was off to the spend a week with a mate who'd moved down that way.

This departure of the eldest and youngest of us, the day after Boxing Day, would prove to be lucky.

When we got home Michael lay down on the floor, ostensibly because his back had gone out but probably also because it was cooler down there. It's always been my practice not to enable the various aches and complaints of the men in my life with excessive sympathy, and so I stepped over him and carried on. And then the signal was sounded, and like a slightly broken Batman, Michael got off the floor, grabbed his gear, and headed off to fight the fire at Ellerslie.

I wasn't, at that stage, particularly worried. Michael had been running off to fires every summer for most of the years we'd been in Batlow. He probably knew what he was doing and I was confident that he wouldn't take any unnecessary risks.

Edmund was another matter. At 18 my son was 10-foot-tall and bulletproof, but I knew that in the Batlow RFS he would be surrounded by older, less reckless, heads. Surely they would keep him from charging into danger.

I spent the day taking down Christmas decorations. When Michael got back that evening, I expected he'd shower and fall into bed; or return to the floor, depending on how his back was faring. Instead, he returned with the news that the fire had gotten away and into the state forest. It was now headed in our direction with nothing to stop it.

And so, Michael and I spent that night outside with knapsacks and handpumps, waiting for the ember attack to begin. We insisted Edmund sleep so he would be rested to start his shift with the RFS at 5 am.

All night the glow of the fire was visible through the trees. All night we watched and waited.

Sulari Gentill

31 December 2019

Shared with Public

Have dropped the dogs into safety in Batlow. Michael and I are fine-tuning pumps ready to defend, while Edmund grabs a couple of hours kip before he heads out with the RFS. The south-western horizon is aglow but no embers yet. This is kinda terrifying. Wish us luck.

About a year later, morning came, and, in the light of day, we thought it was over.

The fire front had gone past us to Kunama. Edmund headed off to chase the flames, and Michael and I spent the day cleaning out gutters, making sure the old Bedford was loaded with pods of water and that the pumps actually worked.

Michael had decided we'd stay and defend. We thought we'd already survived the worst. I posted our survival on my Facebook page.

Around midday Ralph Winter crossed the road to ask us what we were still doing there. Michael told him we were staying. He told us not to be stupid, that Old Tumbarumba Road was done for. As he walked away Michael assured me Ralph was overreacting.

Edmund phoned from the front in Kunama. 'Mum, don't listen to Dad. It's coming. Get the hell outta there!'

Michael laughed when I conveyed the message and told me that Edmund had a penchant for the dramatic.

The police arrived then to inform us that Old Tumbarumba Rd was being closed off — if we stayed we'd be on our own, there would be no help. I remember being quite stunned by the idea that no one would help us. And Michael finally conceded that we were not prepared enough to stay.

I grabbed my laptop, and a couple of changes of clothes. I took my car and three of the dogs, the knapsack and handpump in the front passenger seat in case we encountered spot fires on the road. We couldn't find the cats and we had no way to take the horses.

I posted to Facebook that we were abandoning Grand Oak.

By the time we'd got to Tonkins Bridge at the bottom of Old Tumbarumba Road offers of accommodation were coming in, among them an empty house in Tumut which became our refuge for the next couple of weeks. The Kynastons and the Jones families joined us in that house the next day.

The days that followed waiting for the fire to engulf our town are something of a blur. The Kynastons and the Jones both had dogs so we were dealing with six stressed animals. My dear friend Freda came to the rescue, driving up from Gundagai to take my four hounds back with her, where they would be safe in her fenced yard, looked after and loved. It made life manageable.

Michael and Edmund spent most of their time with the RFS, backburning, fighting, preparing for the day we were told would be the end for Batlow. They'd return to sleep for a few hours and then be off again.

In the house we'd hang off every news report, check the RFS site obsessively, make meals for the RFS. We laughed and joked because that's what we do, but

we all felt brittle. I'd accepted that our wooden house surrounded by bush and undefended, did not stand a chance.

From time to time I'd post on Facebook because it was the easiest way to let friends and family know what was happening, reassure them that we were all right. Those posts were shared and somehow my page became a conduit for concern and solidarity from all over Australia and the world. I spent a lot of time reading messages of support and offers of help, moved by the compassion of friends and strangers alike.

My work was my respite from what was happening. Somewhere in the midst of all that mayhem I received an email and offer of representation from an American literary agent. In other circumstances it would have been something to celebrate madly, in these it was a promise that there was a world on the other side. And so I worked on my new novel, hung on to it as distraction and purpose and hope.

On New Year's Day, I received a message that my house was, as yet, still standing and that it was possible to get back to Batlow via Adelong if you needed to see to stock. I decided to go home. To check on my horses and to say goodbye to my house. I stopped by Coles and bought carrots and apples and drove up, accessing Old Tumbarumba Road via Adelong.

I went straight to the horse paddock with my offering of carrots and apples. I wanted to kiss my ponies one last time and tell them I was sorry; sorry that I couldn't protect them, that there was no way to get them out. But they wouldn't come when I called and I couldn't see them. I hoped they'd found somewhere safe to hide; that somehow they would survive.

The smoke was so thick when I got back to my beloved Grand Oak, I had to hold my breath to run from the car into the house. The power had gone out.

I walked around my house trying to commit as much to memory as possible. I took a couple of paintings off the walls but I felt like I was robbing my own home; and I couldn't choose, I didn't want to choose. I grabbed some things for the boys and called Michael who I knew was somewhere on the fire field to ask him if there was anything he wanted me to salvage. He asked me to grab his great uncle's war diary. Five minutes later he rang back. The reception was scratchy but he was shouting at me to get out of there; the fire had broken the containment lines.

I think it was only that day that I fully realised the enormity of the trouble we were in.

So this morning a friend told me she'd heard my house was still standing and another tipped me off that locals could get through the roadblocks. I secured the hounds here and headed back to check on the horses and to see if it was true. I thought I might be able to get something out at least. At the roadblock they checked my licence and told me, in addition to the expected at your own risk warnings, that I should have a few hours before the wind made things too dangerous again. So I went home. And there it stood in the thick snoke that is suffocating Batlow at the moment. It was surreal and wonderful and exciting to see that Grand Oak still exists...for now at least. I couldn't find the horses...I'm hoping that means they've found a good place to shelter. I left them carrots so they'd know I haven't forgotten them. Then I went back to see what I could load into my car. I stood in the middle of the house overwhelmed at first - how do you choose what part of your life to save? In the end I grabbed the shoebox of receipts (because the Tax office frightens me nearly as much as fire). I also took a few paintings, Edmund's laptop, Atticus' pipe collection, Badger's dog bed and the computer tower...I felt like a thief in my own house. I thought about taking books but there are so many that are precious to me it was like choosing which child to save. So I left their fate in the hands of the house. About five minutes into this exercise I received a call telling me the fire had got away and I had to get out of there immediately. So that was my morning. The chances may be slim but it's still standing.

It was on the morning of the 4th that we noticed that Tumut seemed very quiet. It was eerie. It seemed many people had left. It occurred to us then that Tumut was only 25 minutes from Batlow and that was probably not far enough in the circumstances.

We had no intention of being any further from our husbands and sons than we already were, and so we tried to ready the refuge house, watering down the walls and raking up leaves and debris.

Michael called to tell me the RFS had been pulled back out of Old Tumbarumba Road to protect the town. He expected our house would be gone in 20 minutes.

I was strangely calm in the face of that news. I think I'd said goodbye to the house on New Year's Day, but I could not bear to think about my poor ponies trapped in that Armageddon. I told Michael to keep our son alive.

The Kynastons, the Joneses and I moved into the basement of the refugee house, in the hope a fire would burn over the top of us.

And in the overcrowded heat we listened to the firecoms for any hint of what was going on in Batlow.

We heard the horror, the panic, the resolve and the despair. Hours and hours of fight and flight, grief and fear. Reports that the Batlow Service Station had blown up, gas bottles exploding like popcorn, firies begging for aerial assistance only to be told that the waterbombers were grounded because of the smoke.

The Dunns Road fire roared through Batlow and eventually moved on burning towards Talbingo. The immediate emergency was over. But we had no idea what was left.

In the early hours of the morning, I received a message from Karen Brown, our neighbour. The Browns had defended their property with bulldozers and experience and courage, and so they were still on Old Tumbarumba Road.

Sulari Gentill

5 January 2020

Shared with Public

Michael and Edmund are back...sooty and tired, but fine. And somehow despite the inferno that roared up the hill and turned pyro cumulous on Old Tumbarumba Rd, our house is still standing. The garage which is only a couple of metres from the house, and housed Michael's beloved '52 Vauxhall, all the sheds, the barn, and the boys' cubby are all ashes. Our water tanks all melted as did the trampoline. The garden has been ripped to shreds. And we lost the front fence. But my ponies are fine and Grand Oak is still standing. The next couple of weeks are dangerous because we are now surrounded by smouldering forest which could flare at any time. But we're still here. I think all the good thoughts and hopes you all were sending might have worked. Everything is a crazy mess but now we have a place to start. Xx

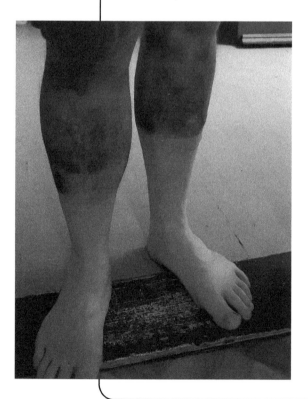

In the days that followed all the roads into Batlow were closed. It was strange post-apocalyptic world, in which the RFS uniform was the only passport. Michael and Edmund went back in to mop up, putting out spot fires and so forth. Between shifts they returned to Grand Oak and took photos — proof of life.

Sulari Gentill

7 January

Shared with Public

I'm still unable to go home and will be for a while but Edmund and Michael were able to check on Grand Oak while putting out spot fires. You can see how close the fire came to the house. The fire front basically crossed at our property so it's amazing there's anything left at all. The flames scorched some walls but didn't catch. The garage and all its contents are gone and, well you can see for yourself. Still, this is fixable! Michael tells me that when it all went to hell on Saturday they were fighting on Posthumous Lane. They were pulled back when the front came in and deployed to Cemetery Road at which point he began to worry about the developing theme!

Sulari Gentill

10 January 2020

Shared with Public

A bright moment while we were trying to secure the house against further ember attack - Edmund compares lenses with a photographer from the New York Times. Looking so forward to the day my boy can go back to spending his spare time taking photos!

They found my horses! Bewildered, frightened but unhurt. Somehow, they had survived the firestorm. To this day, I don't know how. And our singed cat lives!

A day or two later, Edmund took me home. The police were manning all the roadblocks, wary of looters and desperate people who wanted to go home before it was safe, but we were waved through without question.

Old Tumbarumba Road was a smouldering war zone, but in amongst the still-burning trees, the smoke and the ash, my white house stood. It was surreal, unbelievable, wonderful, and appalling at the same time. My garden had been annihilated. The garage, the sheds, the barns were gone. My oak tree was still standing but her canopy and trunk were charred and burned. The entire property was black, every leaf and trunk scorched, every blade of grass gone. We had no fences, no water, no power. It was overwhelming.

I took a moment to mourn what was, to grieve for the garden I'd built with my boys underfoot, the swings and cubbies and history that had been lost.

And then we rolled up our sleeves.

Sulari Gentill

11 January 2020

Shared with Public

Yesterday we got information that the fire could be headed back our way. Atticus and I raced out, bought rakes and saws and drove up to the house to make sure that debris from the last front would not set the house itself alight this time around. The fallen trees had had a couple of days to dry out and would be ample fuel for a new blaze. Michael and Edmund finished their shifts with the RFS and then came out to help.

We eventually got back to our Tumut refuge at 9 pm. The wind had really started to pick up. We'd been back all of 10 minutes when the neighbours rang to let us know the gully behind the barn was alight.

Michael and Edmund headed back immediately. By the time they got there the neighbours had summoned friends with water to douse the fire, but Michael and Edmund stayed the night to ensure there were no further flares. And this morning the house was still standing and the danger had passed.

Atticus and I joined them at the house today to start cleaning up. Darryl from the bottom of the road stopped by in his sidecar contraption to offer us bottled water and warn us about looters. I know. Disasters clearly bring out both the best and worst of humanity.

It was lovely to be home despite the destruction. We rolled up our sleeves and started clearing whatever did not need to be left for insurance assessors. We removed about 10 trees and all the standard roses and we talked about the new garden. We bucketed ashy water from the bottom of melted tanks to save those trees that might still be alive.

Lunch was provided by a group of Sikhs who'd driven from Sydney to feed Batlow and eaten on the verandah amongst the soot. It was rather wonderful.

Despite the fact that the house has neither power nor running water, progress was made. xx

Sulari Gentill

19 January 2020

Shared with Public

So I have been attempting to learn as many lessons as possible from these fires. Aside from the blatantly obvious and overriding message about climate change, I've also been trying to understand why our house didn't burn to the ground. The fact that it's still standing does seem to defy logic.

I think there are a few reasons, but one that is particularly intriguing is the role of this tree. It stands in front the garage which, as you can see, was incinerated. The fire which burned up through the woodlands behind our house to the garage was very hot – so much so that our tanks melted and iron beams buckled into waves. Most of Edmund's tools became a molten mass.

But then it stopped without taking the house.

I think what halted the blaze was this tree – it's a Holm (Evergreen) Oak. Its canopy is so dense that it smoulders rather than catching alight. As you can see the half closest to the garage is burned, and all the leaves are scorched, but it's still standing. And it seems it might have caught the fire and held it rather than sending it on.

The trunk on the side away from the garage looks healthy. When we evacuated, we thought having these trees (which were here when we arrived, five in total) so close to the house meant Grand Oak didn't stand a chance. Now I wonder if they may have been guardians against the flames.

In the fire-affected part of the Trufferie the Holm Oaks seem untouched though Hazels and Roburs have burned.

Anyway, we've decided to give this tree a couple of seasons to recover before we even consider removing it; it's the least we could do.

And I won't be removing the others. In fact I'll be planting a few more as a firebreak. It's probably fanciful but I like the notion that the house was protected by the old oaks which surround it.

The town came home. We greeted friends and neighbours with embraces and, 'So glad you're still here!'

Batlow is a small country town and I used to laugh that it would take us being here another couple of generations to be considered truly Batlownian. But I think Dunns Road made all we 'blow-ins' local.

Online and in life we were inundated with offers of help, and a genuine interest in our recovery. There were government grants for those who'd lost homes and businesses, BlazeAid began to resurrect fences, people raised money and sent gifts. My horses were sent a box of premium apples — the kind that are usually exported to Japan. I received seeds to regrow my lost garden and pyjamas to work in (it seems the fact that I write in pyjamas is not a secret).

The Sikh's arrived to feed the whole town and we were inundated with boxes of supplies from all over the country. The army was sent in which only added to the strange dystopian feel of our post-fire world. NSW Mental Health was also going door to door to see how Batlownians were coping.

To be honest, while I tried to be friendly and reassure them that we were all fine, they would invariably appear while I was working on the novel and take up the precious time I'd reclaimed to write. I recall complaining to Sarah that they kept coming back to my place for some reason.

She laughed. 'Well of course they do. They knock on your door at three in the afternoon and you answer in pyjamas. They probably think you're depressed!'

And so I started getting dressed to fend off Mental Health.

Sulari Gentill

14 January 2020

Shared with Public

This is what popping in to get a few things looks like now... milk, bread and a bale of hay. My little yellow car has earned her stripes as a rural work horse! I owe her a bit of a detail when this is all over! But a huge thank you to the emergency fodder people who gave me this bale to keep my poor ponies fed until grass grows again.

Arrived home to find the tree in front of our house was on fire. That's the thing right now. So many trees are smouldering, the giant gums could all have roots on fire though the trunks seem cold; a quiet subterranean threat that takes on monster proportions the moment it finds oxygen. We'll be putting out these spot fires for months.

But for now, (and because this fire was beyond our current backpack firefighting equipment) I have firies on speed dial.

The power is now on at home. Hats off to the #Essential Energy who worked day and night to restore it well before anyone thought it possible. It means we can move back home and watch for spot fires among other things. Thank you, guys.

Have also collected my hounds from Gundagai where they were being protected and loved by Freda Marnie, while I lived in Tumut in a house loaned by the Manning family. So many people have been so kind throughout this crisis. Through the haze of smoke, we've seen the very best of Australians. Xx

Sulari Gentill

30 January 2020

Shared with Public

At midnight we woke to an almighty crack – like thunder but slightly different in tone. Because our bedroom is now in the shadow of several half-burnt gum trees, Michael and I got up immediately to investigate. And so we first saw this by torch light.

The grand oak after which our property is named, for which I agreed to move to Batlow in the first place, from the branches of which we hung swings and pushed our boys into the air, under whose shade we celebrated each birthday, which had stopped the fire which came from from the north and seemed to be recovering.

My beautiful 100-year oak tree.

An ember must have been sucked into the delta of its branches (I know delta's not the right word but you know what I mean). It burned away enough to split my beloved tree. Am calling in the tree surgeons to see if she can be saved but it doesn't look good. She's lost more than 50% of her crown – the part that was regenerating most vigorously. Just yesterday we were celebrating her new leaves. Still, nobody was hurt. Without our garages the boys have been working on cars beneath her canopy. That this happened in the middle of the night was lucky. But I can't imagine this place without her.

Sulari Gentill

24 March 2020

Shared with Public

Last weekend the tree surgeons came in to deal with the copse of old pines across the road. About 30 metres tall, they had been fire impacted and deemed dangerous. I lamented the execution order, because I like trees and I have known these old giants personally for twenty years, and lately it seems I have been saying goodbye a lot. The surgeons began by removing all the limbs to make felling the trunks safer. They worked with chainsaws and elevation platforms for two days. Every time the chainsaws stopped there'd be a crack and a crash and another great limb would fall. They had de-limbed most of the trees when someone found a bit of asbestos beneath one (a plank of fibro I think). Of course the work stopped immediately and the surgeons have not returned. It looks a little like a modern art installation – not Blue Poles but Burnt Poles.

I was up just after dawn this morning and glanced at the black silhouettes with a twinge of sadness for the trees, and I noticed that for the first time I can see the mountains behind them and the sun rise over the horizon. And it occurred to me that as we are all watching life as we know it being de-limbed, perhaps we will see mountains and daybreak in the space that is made. Hang in there everybody. I know things are getting rough, but there will be light on the other side. xx

Sulari Gentill

27 February 2020

Shared with Public

So, I've spent part of this morning wrestling and cursing the lawn mower which only survived the bushfire because I forgot to put it away in the garage. It does seem to me that not starting is a particularly ungrateful way of repaying my life-saving negligence. After pulling the cord repeatedly for 30 minutes I checked the fuel tank. It was empty. And sadly, while I forgot to put the mower away, I did return all the fuel canisters to their rightful place in the garage, which now looks like this (below).

(When I got home yesterday, I found some vandal had come in and spray-painted it, its contents, and every other ruin on the property, pink. I suspect the government).

So my mowing plans are thwarted, but at least it gives me a perfect excuse to spend the day writing and watching Netflix... Cue, a call from Michael made from his office landline. It seems he grabbed the remote control instead of his phone when he left for work today. And the stupid smart TV does not have buttons. And before anybody asks, Michael has an iPhone, it looks nothing like the remote control. But I might have to have the government spray-paint one or the other pink just to make that clear.

[Editor's note: The pink spray paint was a mixture of glue and paint applied to sites which contained asbestos]

Sulari Gentill

2 August 2020

Shared with Public

We're cleaning up the piles of burnt trees in the house paddock. Ironically the only way to remove the remains is to burn them.

There are a lot of pine trees in the heaps which burn fast and hot (as we saw in January) so Edmund is spending the night on bonfire duty. Luckily he's been watching Yellowstone, and has gone cowboy again.

Sulari Gentill

7 August 2020

Shared with Public

I pulled into the driveway a few minutes ago to find my beloved wounded oak tree had, in the hour I'd been away, succumbed to the wind. And I too am broken...I knew this was possible but I dared to believe she was going to come good. I can't imagine my garden without her. She's watched over us all these years.

Sulari Gentill

16 August 2020

Shared with Public

The garden today...it looks like the scene of a battle, which I suppose it was. But it won't always be this way. In a few months these will just be the before shots.

Sulari Gentill

22 August 2020

Shared with Public

This photo tells the story of 2020

Sulari Gentill

7 November 2020 ·

Shared with Public

Today, Atticus and I planted a Mt Fuji standard ornamental cherry tree into the burned-out stump of the monster tree. It grows out like an umbrella rather than weeping. The bobcats came in to finally clear the last of fire debris from the yard and put back some topsoil so that I can begin seeding grass. Then I suppose I'll have to spend the rest of the year trying to keep the cockatoos and galahs from eating my lawn.

The two years since the fire have been a slow and steady return.

Fire debris cleared, water pipes replaced, out-buildings rebuilt, lawn reseeded. Planting hundreds of trees to replace the lost giants.

Dunns Road's tail has been long, and it's had a sting. Trees we thought had survived proved mortally wounded, dying slowly even as we scrambled to save them.

The landscape is changed, the contours naked and visible. There are new views, fresh scars on the hills.

Batlow has been the beneficiary of solidarity and kindness from all over the world. Thousands of shoulders offered on which we could lean. For me this was what I remember most.

We remain a tiny town nestled in the foothills of the Snowy Mountains but are no longer, nor will ever again be, as remote as we once were.

Sulari Gentill

11 November 2020

Shared with Public

I've been keeping this under my hat for a few days because I didn't want to get hopes up – mine or yours – but now I think I can safely say, the Grand Oak lives!

Even like this, she is beautiful and one day I'll stand in her shade again! I am in awe of the quiet, magnificent resilience of trees.

The photographs in Undefendable were taken by the townsfolk of Batlow and visiting volunteers, during the Black Summer bushfires of 2019-20 and over the many months of recovery since.

The Blenkins/Gentill family
pages: 8, 28, 30. 33. 36, 37, 39, 50, 65, 69, 80, 83, 86, 89, 90, 94, 97, 99, 100, 103, 104,, 125, 138, 142, 143, 148, 154-171

The Watkins family
pages: 124, 173

The Cross family
pages: 126, 128, 129

The Brown family
Cover photos, and pages: 6, 16, 29, 47, 57, 67, 70, 72, 77, 135, 144

The Ironside family
pages: 34, 109, 110, 114, 117

Fred Fairlie
pages: 13, 14, 15, 19

Kate Masterson
pages: 9, 24, 60, 62, 92, 93, 107, 119, 146, 150

Wayne Dubois
pages: 41, 44

Anne Hallard
pages: 52, 53, 54, 55

Joe McGirr
page: 132

The Singh family
Guru Nanak's Free Kitchenette Sydney
pages: 121, 122, 136, 161